STRONG WOMEN, FED-UP MEN, DEFEATED SONS, BROKEN DAUGHTERS

HEALING GENERATIONAL PAIN

MARK MOMPLAISIR

ACKNOWLEDGEMENT

When I first started writing this book, I was both nervous and excited. Writing a book was new, and it was scary to me. I want to thank everyone who cheered for me and helped facilitate this process. Special thanks to my clients who indulged in all of our conversations. To my friends who allowed me to hear their thoughts, and for being open to hearing mine--thank you. To my editors, who are everything to this book--thank you so much. I have so many people to thank, that naming everyone individually would take another book. I want you all to know that you are special to me, and that I'm forever grateful for every moment, every inspiration, and every word of motivation I get to share with you all. To Mom and Dad: I love you both more than words could ever express, even when I don't say it often enough. Thank you loving me the way you do and for always praying for me. To my brothers: You are all everything, and I'm super proud of every single one of you. To everyone who has provided a safe space for me to share all of my not-so-conventional ideas about health and fitness, healing and living purposefully. You are my MVPs, and I am indebted to you for your ability to serve others and me, wholeheartedly and without expectations for getting anything in return. To the little girl who brings me life and makes everything colorful: Ariella, I love you more and more every day, and I'm grateful for you and your mom for making me a dad. You're the smartest, kindest, funniest, sweetest, most beautiful human being in the world, and I wish you could only see yourself through my eyes every second of your life. You are the most precious part of my purpose. I love you to infinity and beyond. And to everyone who reads this book: I pray that it is instrumental to your healing journey and that it propels you to live a fulfilling, peaceful, and purpose-filled life.

TABLE OF CONTENTS

INTRODUCTION

The idea for this book started with my curiosity to learn and to understand African history and how it impacts every aspect of our lives, and a desire to help, heal, and create change in one person, one family, and one community at a time. Conversations with friends, colleagues, and clients often led to heated discussions about family dynamics and generational habits. My goal was to learn how to get out of my own way, my own feelings, my own head, and my own emotions and start changing my life. By examining the history of my people, I became aware of pervasive detrimental habits, destructive mindsets, and unhealthy patterns in my life and in those around me. This book is about breaking generational patterns that have kept us in bondage mentally, emotionally, and spiritually. It's about understanding where we came from, who we are, and who we are meant to be. It's about healing and living a life that is filled with kindness, self-love, self-care, love for one another, gratitude, grace, honesty, purpose and peace of mind.

I begin with a brief history of the African people, including slavery and its residual destructive habits, customs, and teachings that keep us down and count us out. Slavery created psychological traumas that have been passed down from generation to generation through pain, a false sense of mental strength, and a lack of emotional and spiritual connections between parents and children. History shines a light on the disparity of mental health awareness in African-descent communities and how the lack of adequate health services has torn these communities apart. Each chapter addresses the damaging cycle that creates generations of hurt and emotionally wounded parents who raise their children to continue the cycle of brokenness. The way we love, treat, and see ourselves and each other throughout most of the African-descent countries clearly shows the destructive psychological effects of slavery. It is essential that we learn from our history and find ways to heal, forgive, and live a purposeful life. It is only through forgiveness and awareness that we will learn to see and treat each other with grace, appreciation, and purpose.

Like me, I hope you will learn new habits and get rid of some of the detrimental behaviors that keep us stuck, depressed, anxious, unfulfilled, and empty, and start finding new ways to break the cycle of disappointment, anger, and high expectations. As a coach, mentor, and mental health and wellness advocate, I've heard stories and shared laughs, tears, disappointments, and joy with many people who are on the quest of finding inner peace and life purpose. Their struggle inspired me to share my story and experiences. Prayerfully, through my story and those shared by others in the book, you too can learn how to heal your brokenness, your wounds, your past hurts, and your disappointments and find the path to greatness. Through these words, I hope you find healing, and that you're able to use your experiences as vessels and gateways for someone else's healing. Holding on to past hurts can justify our anxiety and fury. But remember, you deserve peace of mind and a life filled with purpose.

I pray you find healing in the things and the people whom you weren't ready to forgive and receive forgiveness from. Above all, I pray you find the wisdom to recognize your truths, face your truths, heal from your truths, forgive your truths, and lastly, start living your newfound truths.

CHAPTER 1

AFRICAN EXPERIENCES

IT IS DIFFICULT TO KNOW what came first: the mindset and modern misfortune that we were born into or the results of our long-lived captivity that got us to where we are as children of Africa. I recall taking an African American-experience course in college that shook my mind, body, and soul. Being from the Caribbean, my knowledge about slavery was limited to what our colonizers taught us. We were taught that Haiti was "discovered" by the exploiter, Christopher Columbus, and how we fought the French and became independent. But the understanding of how we became who we are, including how we love and treat one another, weren't lessons from our history but from those who invaded our country. The truth is that living in bondage for hundreds of years affected us, producing psychological trauma that is still with us. Our self-destructive mindsets, our unhealthy habits, our inconsistent cultural patterns, our strengths, our weaknesses all exist in the basic foundation of our fundamental teachings, traditions, and generational patterns, which many of us find ourselves fighting to break away from. Our psychological suffering in the Americas, and nearly every African-descent country, is proof that the damaging effect of slavery is far greater than we can ever imagine.

Self-Understanding

The history of the African people began with exploitation, kidnapping, and slavery. During slavery, African-descent mothers, fathers, and children were not allowed to live together and have family traditions—such as dinner, stories, and other gatherings—because they were the property of their masters. Men would work in the fields from sunup to sundown, seven days a week, barely fed, beaten, dying from illnesses and hunger, while the women were domestic workers taking care of the children, cleaning and cooking, being sexually exploited and forced to be impregnated by their own sons and relatives for the purpose of producing more slaves. For hundreds of years, African-descent men, women, and children were auctioned to other slave owners as laborers and tools, beaten and abused continuously. The life that our ancestors were brought into had to be endured, and many died knowing there was no end in sight for the children they left behind. African-descent men felt powerless and useless because they were unable to defend their women and children against the brutality of their masters. Witnessing their entire family begging for mercy while being raped and demoralized day in and day out, and not being able to help, was physically, spiritually, and psychologically destructive. Imagine watching your beautiful African-descent queens being used as exhibits and experiments, treated mercilessly, and there was absolutely nothing you could do to put an end to it. But you got through it. You endured it. You survived it. You African-descent kings never had the chance to become men because you were seen as boys, peasants, inferior animals. You held onto your anger and pain because you couldn't stand up to your masters, look them in their eyes, and show them how you really felt. And if one of you ever had the courage to protest, you'd be hanged, sodomized, beaten, whipped, or killed. Our ancestors went through this. Whether it was in Haiti, Jamaica, or the United States, the physically strong African-descent kings got through these dark times. You endured days, weeks, and months chained up in ships sailing across the Atlantic Ocean—hungry, sick, stolen from your family and your loved ones, not knowing where you were going and how bad your life was going to be. You breathed through that.

Then one day, you were told by society you needed to be a man. It didn't matter if you were twelve or fifty years old, you were expected to be a man. From the ashes of your ancestors, who were never taught what it meant to be a man, you were expected to protect, provide, and take care of your family. When you no longer worked the fields and African-descent women and children were no longer the property of their masters, you refused to be the little boy that you were still called, even if you were nearly sixty years old. With no education and no skills other than the plantation labor, with no land or property of your own, your women, daughters, and sons became your responsibility. It was up to you now, African-descent men, to embark on this new journey of being a free man with nothing. It was you, African-descent boys, who endured the pain and confusion of seeing the men who were supposed to be your role models tossed away. You were left wondering if your life would be different. It was you, African-descent women, who found yourselves raising families you didn't create on your own, taking on the responsibility to protect and provide for them in spite of the lack of resources. African-descent girls felt empty and wounded because they too deserved to feel the love of their fathers and mothers that they couldn't dare to ask for. But, somehow, someway, you made it through. Broken and shattered. Lost and filled with despair. Fighting for what was right. Beaten for being alive. Spat on because of the color of your skin. Dying for freedom. Shamed in a place you never asked to be brought to. But you were still alive, striving, fighting, and hoping to one day be seen for the gift that you truly are.

Our Disarmament

When we think of being disarmed, most of us automatically think of battlefields, wars, and demilitarization. We think of being stripped of our powers, weapons, and being neutralized. But in our communities and African-descent countries, the disarmament of our African-descent families was the residual servitude mindset that came from a lack of knowledge of our history and self-worth.

Weaponizing ourselves for our own self-destruction was the tactic used by our oppressors. We have been divided and conquered by the attitude that we are and have always been inferior to European and Western civilization. In spite of our advancement in arts, technology, medicine, and astronomy prior to Western civilization, somehow we have been convinced to see past our greatness. We were taught that our complexion, our hair, our noses, our bodies, and our minds were inferior. We have been so discombobulated by Western civilization, blinded by materialistic fantasies, that we have lost sight of the ethical values, traditions, and belief systems that our ancestors stood and died for. Be it Africa, Haiti, or any other African-offspring countries, we have been used and exploited for our own self-obliteration, killing ourselves, hating ourselves, and pulling each other down for reasons that serve none of us. We have been used against ourselves because of our weaknesses and need for equality.

I recall a conversation I had with a colleague about the structural paradigm of many African-descent families. For as long as I can remember, the belief among our families is that the woman is always right. While some of you might disagree, I've always believed this was an insult to smart, emotionally mature women as a whole. To think and say that someone is always right is like saying that she is not emotionally established enough to understand or handle viewpoints that differ from her own. I have seen African-descent men who would rather be "yes, dear" type of men in order to maintain the peace in their household, which again reinforces the belief that women cannot reason and should be avoided, rather than disagree with them or get on their bad side. As a result, we have created traditions and cultures that have led to our own destruction.

One of the goals of our oppressors was to keep African-descent families divided, by breaking down the men's spirit and giving the women a sense of control. Creating a domineering matriarchal system, which they have no respect for, serves the agenda of women being in control. Break down, kill, and imprison the African-descent men, and let their sons grow up in households without fathers, in the belief that mothers don't need them. But what we have been creating is a cycle of self-destruction. I am not disparaging mothers who have persevered despite the cards they have been dealt and the cultures that have been created for them, but if we can't pause and look at ourselves in the mirror, take accountability for our shortcomings and our own ignorance, we'll keep creating generations of men that our daughters will need to run for cover from. Men who have no idea what their true purpose is and what being a man should be. We'll keep raising men who will continuously find themselves too busy fighting to be loved and accepted by the women they choose, while missing out on their life's purpose. Generations of men who have no idea how to be responsible men, fathers, and companions. We'll continue to raise sensitive and charismatic men who know how to love every woman they set eyes on, but have no idea how to love and respect one woman. We'll keep raising men who have no idea how to be leaders, innovators, and providers. We'll raise men who will endlessly pay for their fathers' sins, men who will refuse to be like their fathers but have no idea how to be anything or anyone else.

Likewise, we'll keep raising generations of women who keep getting hurt and broken by the thinking that it is normal to create this imbalanced family dynamic of raising sons and daughters on their own and continue to create generations of wounded and fragile children. Women who keep getting hurt by the same men that were raised by them and continue to say they are "no good men"—but fail to accept that those men didn't raise themselves. We'll keep raising women who will keep raising daughters to be like their mothers, broken and blinded by their mothers' pain. We'll keep raising women who have no clue what it means to be a woman because their mothers didn't know how to teach them. And because we are not being taught what a family structure should be, we'll continue to be at the bottom of society, where we are disrespected, killed, imprisoned, hurt, and broken.

If we are not willing to create healthy family paradigms, if we are too busy fighting one another and blaming each other for the things that most of us have no idea how to do, we'll never unite; we'll never gain enough courage to create our own paths, voices, markets, plans, lifestyles, and productive communities. If as parents we are not willing to teach our sons and daughters what it means to be men and women, we'll always find ourselves lost and confused and quick to follow everything that is trending or popular. This is not an attack on the African-descent woman or the African-descent man. It's a revelation of our demise as the African-descent people, a call for healing and restoration. We've created a matriarchal dynamic where strong women are raising strong girls who don't need men, but those same women are raising sensitive boys to grow up to be men who depend on the women who don't need them. Boys who grow up doing everything to impress the same women who don't need them, spending time and energy trying to impress them because we're not being taught how to love each other. We're raising men who are more concerned with flashy rims and shiny jewelry than standing up for a cause of humanity. We are raising men that our daughters will call "ain't shit men" and "deadbeat dads," partly because we're not willing to face our reality. We're too afraid to hurt each other's feelings by acknowledging that children need their fathers as much as they need their mothers, so we encourage dysfunctional behaviors and refuse to take accountability. As men, we've chosen to be more concerned with being liked and accepted, profiting off of saying what sounds good and pretty to the ears and leaving our African-descent women to raise our children alone.

Until we face that reality, until we're no longer afraid to take accountability and responsibility for ourselves, respect will never be earned. Until we understand the role of our men, our women, our mothers, and our fathers, nothing will ever change. It's time to start seeing each other differently if we want things to change. If we want our sons and daughters to have a better shot at being emotionally and spiritually healthy, whole, respected, and heard. If we want our children to stand up for causes that make our society better, not just for themselves but for future generations to come, we need to create a better dynamic for them to model. We must teach by example.

Our Disengagement

When I envision what my people went through, I can see and feel their pain. I empathize with the psychological brokenness children of Africa endure. I imagine myself in a place that is filled with evil and darkness, cruelty and abuse. Endless sufferings that would eventually break down the sanctified bond between the African-descent man and the African-descent woman. Even after the abolition of slavery, the Black Codes and Jim Crow segregation continued to keep you dejected. Despite getting up on your feet, educating yourself, creating businesses, and providing for your family, the oppressors came along and destroyed your efforts, burned down your homes, killed your families, and stopped you from voting and holding public office.

You were controlled and manipulated by a system that was never designed to serve you. Kings and queens became three-fifths of a person with no human rights and no way to provide for themselves and their families. The African-descent woman and the African-descent man found themselves unable to make sense of their new life. The African-descent woman had to keep working for pennies or food as a housekeeper, a maid, and a servant because the African-descent man couldn't make enough to care for his family as a sharecropper. Like many of my African-descent brothers, I worry about not being able to provide and protect myself and my family, and it hurts deeply.

It's in a man's genetic material to protect and provide for his family, but the African-descent man was failing at both. You, African-descent queen, became the main—and sometimes the sole—breadwinner in the family. But you were busy raising your oppressors' children, you had no time to raise your own, and Dad was never taught about raising children—all he knew was working the fields. Your children were raising themselves with little guidance, no education, no proper home training, and no one to model what love and family should be like. Once again, you faced the cycle of destruction passed down from generation to generation.

As time went by, poverty and hunger conquered the African-descent communities. The same system that convinced the African-descent woman that the African-descent man was useless, pretended to be the salvation of the African-descent communities. The welfare system, which included public housing projects, essentially encouraged the African-descent woman to get rid of the African-descent man if she and her children were to be eligible for those public assistances. It was another way to disarm the African-descent family and gain control of their communities, annihilate the men, give the children no options and opportunities for a better life. If the African-descent man can't provide and protect, what good is he to the woman and the children? The system is ready to help as long as they maintain control. We'll give you assistance, but the African-descent man in your life has got to go.

This destructive cycle has kept African-descent men unemployed, uneducated, lost, and frustrated. The self-hate, the defeat, and the frustration are pervasive. Families are vulnerable because Dad left us alone, or he was a nobody, as Mom was made to believe. But you, African-descent man, are equally alone, searching for a way to survive. To allegedly protect those projects and keep everyone at bay, cops patrol the projects—but instead of protecting the community, the police are there to protect others *from* you. If you act up out of anger and frustration, their job is to quickly remind you who you are and where you belong. You get arrested and thrown in jail and become a felon. And as a criminal, your chance of finding a job has become drastically diminished. There goes your future and the future of your sons following in your footsteps.

Mama can't teach your sons to be men, so their friends did. Now Mom is forced to become strong because she has to play the roles of

Mom and Dad. She becomes protector and provider, counselor and caregiver, but she never has had a chance to heal her own wounds. Your son becomes defeated because there is no way out, and nothing he does at this point will change the course of his destiny. By the time he reaches manhood, he becomes tired and fed up.

As an adolescent, he thinks he knows what it means to be a man and he starts displaying attributes of what he thinks a man is and does. He starts finding ways to survive and make a living with all the guns that are being brought into his community. He might start selling drugs that were brought into his community by the very people who have abused and oppressed his ancestors. Many youths find themselves hanging with groups of friends who share their hurt and their understanding of what being a man is all about. They believe that they are becoming real men by being destructive and dysfunctional. Those who do not end up dead or in jail might be pushed out of their community by gentrification.

Our daughters become broken watching Mommy work multiple jobs, selling her soul and still struggling to make ends meet. They are hurt and frustrated knowing it shouldn't have been Mom's job to raise them all alone. Depression, lack of self-esteem, emptiness, suicidal thoughts, promiscuity, and drugs are part of their world. And the question that keeps running through their mind is where's Daddy? So they replace Daddy with another defeated boy, who never had the chance to be a boy and who grew up too fast. A defeated boy who now thinks he's a man—and they produce more broken girls and defeated boys…and so the cycle of strong women, fed-up men, broken girls, and defeated boys continues.

CHAPTER 2

STRONG WOMEN, FED-UP MEN, DEFEATED BOYS, AND BROKEN GIRLS

IT'S ALWAYS SURPRISING, AND SOMEWHAT miraculous in our communities, to say that your biological parents are happily married and still together. And I'm not talking about walking-on-the-opposite-side-of-the-streets-because-they-can't-stand-being-next-to-each-other kind of together, or staying-together-because-of-the-children kind of together. I'm talking about being together by walking the same path, creating memories, respecting, valuing, and appreciating each other's sacrifices and all the little things they do to make each other's life more meaningful, and being good and loving examples to their children. It is something that I didn't get to experience. Something that the majority of our African-descent children and families did not, do not, and will not experience until we start analyzing our detrimental habits, heal ourselves from our ancestors' wounds, and change our mindsets.

It's disheartening to see how our society praises African-descent women for being single mothers even when they are struggling to raise children on their own. This kind of attitude promotes brokenness and systemically cheers on the dysfunction of African-descent families. Shouldn't we praise and encourage healthy-relationship households instead? Even more disturbing are emotionally and psychologically unprepared young men and women having children and passing down generational dysfunctions and damaging habits, blaming one another instead of taking accountability for themselves. In a way, we as adults are fighting against each other, creating more divisions while our broken daughters and defeated sons learn our unproductive ways and become adult versions of ourselves.

In our African-descent households and families, boys are expected to prematurely become men and consequently feel defeated by their inability to function as men. Girls are feeling lost and unloved, relying on physical gratification to define their self-worth and on broken promises in order to feel whole. When women don't let their childhood brokenness and their accumulated pain overpower their strength, they push through the hurt and disappointment, sacrificing their healing process. Because it's not in their DNA to give up, they're forced to wave their strength as banners.

Similarly, men are fed up with heavy expectations from their childhood that they have yet to meet. They are fed up with societal definitions of manhood that they are failing to uphold. They are fed up with daily reminders of their inability to be good and romantic husbands and partners, good providers, great protectors, caring sons, law-abiding citizens, and upstanding human beings.

Sons and daughters are burdened by having to grow up too quickly and become adults, bypassing their childhood because they are being seen and treated as adults. But it is not too late to change course. We have reached the time where we, as adults, can start our own healing process and become healthier and whole.

Apprehended Mindsets

Although it's not impossible, it's extremely difficult to know what you were never taught. As children we are consciously and subconsciously whom our parents (and our history as slaves) taught us to be. We are the by-products of slavery. But just as we can learn to work towards our purpose to become who we were meant to be as adults, we can also learn to reject the slavery mentality and become who we were meant to be as descendants of Africa. We have been told that slavery ended years ago and that we should forget about it, but can we ever forget the way our parents raised us? Regardless of how old you live to be, the memories, the traditions, the habits, the dysfunctions, and the hurt that we may have inherited from our parents never go away.

Imagine not being able to have your own beliefs or practice your faith. Imagine not feeling protected and loved by the people who were created to care for you and support you physically, emotionally, and spiritually. How do you learn how to be who you were meant to be? How did you learn what loving an African-descent man looks like? How did you learn what loving an African-descent woman should be like? How do you learn what loving your children looks like? Most of us still love each other the way that our masters loved us—with whips and chains. The abuse we experienced is now expressed in verbal put-downs, physical violence, and unappreciation.

We see each other and ourselves with the eyes of our oppressors. We talk to each other with the tongues of our masters, by calling each other derogatory names and being unsupportive and envious of one another. We treat each other the same way our ancestors were treated by their owners, only now we use guns and social media outlets. And although we crave each other's love and acceptance, we've been taught to destroy our sisters and brothers. We've been taught to depreciate each other's values and morals because we don't see each other as beautiful enough, as strong enough, as loving enough, as wealthy enough, as with skin not light or dark enough. How do you accept and love others who look like you, talk like you, and live like you when you were never taught to accept and love yourself? How do you treat others who are like you with kindness and respect when you were always made to believe that something is wrong with you? So you find it easier to hate each other. To see each other as the enemy because it's easier to stay divided that way. It's easier to hold on to what we were taught and the belief that we are each other's disgrace.

Self-Minimization

I have been in interracial relationships and truly believe whoever understands you, helps you maintain your peace, walk with you towards achieving your purpose, evolves with you, sacrifices for you, and appreciates your sacrifices can share your love. It's no longer about Black, White, Asian, Hispanic or anything else, if you have healed from the ancestral trauma of slavery and oppression and can love each other wholeheartedly. However, our perceptions of each other dictate how we treat and or act towards one another. For example, the African-descent man's perception of the European-descent woman may be that she's less aggressive, less argumentative, less confrontational, and more feminine than the African-descent woman. He might enter into a less guarded relationship with the European-descent woman, with fewer expectations, and treat that woman differently than he would the African-descent woman. He'll have more patience, sympathy, and fewer fears, but, nevertheless, he'll still crave the love of the African-descent woman. The African-descent woman's perception of the European-descent man may be that he's more financially able, more respectful, a better caretaker of his family, and more authoritative, and he does not ask for as much in the relationship. She'll be less guarded and more respectful. The feelings African-descent men and African-descent women have towards one another have been extremely distorted, because we were trained to magnify each other's perceived deficiencies. We think less of each other because of the images that have been portrayed about us and the resentments we have accumulated, because we do not know how to love ourselves and appreciate each other. We amplify our sense of worthiness by comparing and diminishing someone else who resembles us.

The culture and traditions of our oppressors have led African-descent ethnic groups to diminish each other's worthiness. For similar reasons, we get into relationships with each other with negative preconceived ideas, hurtful habits, and a deficiency in emotional health and expect the African-descent man or the African-descent woman to fix those deep psychologically rooted traumas. It's easier to pretend to be better, kinder, more loving, and happier with someone else, because we subconsciously lay our burdens on those who look like us and are able to relate to our struggles. It's not that the African-descent man and the African-descent woman don't love one another and can't be better mates to one another; it's simply that our emotional dependency and expectations are unreasonably high, which causes chaos when we each fail to meet them.

Another problem is that we don't seek to understand our brokenness and heal our psychological traumas before engaging in relationships with each other (the reminder of the sources of your hurt). When we carry our past hurts, be they romantic or parental, into new relationships, the result can be dysfunctional. We've allowed our undesirable perceptions of one another to dictate how we view ourselves—with hate, unworthiness, shamefulness, and subordination. Until we start seeing ourselves with positivity and a sense of worthiness, we'll continue to degrade one another and pull each other down.

Rooted Resentment

Understanding the psychological, emotional, and spiritual damage caused by slavery doesn't require a high level of education. The African-descent men and the African-descent women were made for each other. This is not meant to dismiss interracial relationships or biracial children; those are mainly byproducts of slavery and Western social reconstruction. Prior to slavery and Western civilization, the African man's life purpose was to protect, love, cherish, and provide for the African woman and help her raise their children. Likewise, the life purpose of the African woman was to protect, provide, support, and love the African man. What happened when the African-descent woman was in pain and being abused and the African-descent man couldn't protect her? What happened when the African-descent man was being mentally, spiritually and physically broken down and the African-descent woman couldn't provide any support to him? What happened when your sons had to work the fields alongside you, hungry, sick, beaten from sunup to sundown and you couldn't say or do anything to protect them? What happened when your daughters were being used and impregnated, abused and raped, and you couldn't do anything to help them? What happened? Are you mad at each other? Do you resent each other? Who taught us how to see, treat, and understand each other and our history? In whose eyes are we seeing each other?

If the very same person that was created for you was right there with you, witnessing your agony but still couldn't do anything to help you, wouldn't you be resentful, angry, disappointed, hurt at some point? Eventually, some of us will start aligning our values with our abusers because we do not see a way out; and when hope runs out, survival instincts kick in and it becomes either surrender and accept your fate or fight in spite of the high possibility of failing. After over four hundred years of brokenness, beating, abuse, and disconnect, one cannot expect to just wake up one day and have it all figured out. All the hurt, anger, disappointment, pain, nightmares, killings, lynching, financial disparities, and social isolation don't magically disappear. They require awareness. They require conscious acknowledgment and the decision to find healing and create new healthier mindsets. They require forgiveness, not only for the African-descent men and women who couldn't protect and provide for their loved ones, but, more importantly, for oneself.

Forgiving oneself for having gone through the traumatic experiences that left you empty, broken, and resentful. Forgiving oneself for blaming and crucifying those who went through and are still going through the same struggles as you. We weren't taught better. We don't know better and most of us are still learning and practicing habits that create dysfunction and generational chaos.

The Fed-Up Man

As I said earlier, if there was one thing that the African-descent man was taught, it was how not to be a man. He was never seen as a man and was never given the chance to be a man. In spite of his biological and innate abilities to be masculine and function as a man, he was either beaten, subdued into submissiveness, or stripped away of everything that defined him as a man. As children we learn by example and our natural genetic instincts. If you grow up and all you see is hard labor and abuse, all you will learn is hard labor and abuse. You have all the right instincts to provide and protect, to hustle and get more, but you were never taught why and how. You worked for your masters; it's what you were supposed to do. It was your purpose—to them, it was what you were created for. You could never work hard enough. You could never be too tired enough; you could never be too hungry enough. Your purpose was to work, produce more slaves, work some more, or get whipped or killed. There was no such thing as being a loving husband, father, and man. Living such a life doesn't teach, encourage, and propel positive lifestyles or behavior. Post slavery, it was still nearly impossible for you to provide and protect because that would require you to have a voice, a job, options, laws to protect you, and a family to support your decisions. How do you do those things when you were never taught by your parents, who were also enslaved? You still have to fight for justice and racial acceptance; you still have to fight not to be imprisoned. This kind of psychological discrepancy is difficult to overcome without conscious awareness and holistic healing.

African-descent boys, African-descent men, your spirit has been broken; you've become lost, confused, defeated, and fed up. If it's not just the system that was built against you judicially, financially, and psychologically, it's your own brothers aiming their anger and misguided pain towards you. It's your own self-hate tearing you down, destroying you emotionally and mentally. It's your own household ripping you apart when you fail to meet expectations and societal standards. It's your lack of guidance and opportunities that left you vulnerable and easily preyed on. It's your complexion that makes you a target and a danger to Western civilization. It's your weaknesses and hunger to fit in that causes you to lose sight of who you were meant to be and who is fighting alongside you.

Although these things may have been preordained for you, they are not your purpose and definitely not your destiny or who you were created to be. You are responsible for picking yourself up, picking each other up, raising your children, learning your history, understanding it, and becoming who you were meant to be.

The Strong Woman

When you apply enough pressure on a muscle, that force tears apart those muscle fibers, either causing them to be injured or to become stronger. When most African-descent women encounter pressure, they may fold, they may bend, but they become stronger. Even if they tumble and fall, they get up, dust themselves off and become stronger than ever before. As commendable as that sounds, it all comes at a price: the expectations, the hurt, the loneliness, the heavy load of raising children alone, the nurturing, the caretaking, the neglect of oneself. Starting from slavery, the African-descent women were in charge of raising the children and taking care of the home—not necessarily their own children and homes, but it was part of their purpose. They were never taught how to be women or mothers to their own children, let alone how to love the African-descent man; their purpose was to be the property of their masters and the masters' needs. They were taught to love, obey, and submit to their masters.

As I mentioned, African-descent men and African-descent women were never taught how to be with each other and love each other. However, we crave each other and our biological instincts understand that we were created for each other. When slavery ended, we were able to openly have the family that we longed for, but we were never taught *how* to have it. We never witnessed it from our parents, so we had no idea how to do it and how to maintain it healthily. The African-descent man, who was already defeated and fed up from being told by his master that he never worked hard enough or was never docile enough, was suddenly faced with the task of supporting and protecting his wife and children.

The African-descent woman, who survived the struggles, the abuses, and the hard labors of serving her master's wife, had yet to learn the definition of womanhood. Inevitably, the African-descent man, who had no idea how to be the Western man that she craved, once again fell short. The result is disappointment and rejection for both the African-descent man and the African-descent woman. The African-descent woman starts taking on more work in order to provide for herself and her children, rejects the African-descent man, and disrespects him because he doesn't measure up to what she has been told that a man should be. When he doesn't make enough money and is unable to provide the lifestyle she was told she deserves, she becomes independent and strong, doing it all on her own.

The African-descent man gets more fed up because he feels inadequate and searches for quick and easy ways to make a buck so he can regain his manhood. If he fails, he will either be kicked out of the house by the strong woman, or he will decide to leave in the hope of finding peace of mind. But neither the African-descent man nor the African-descent woman is thinking about their sons and daughters. Our psychological, emotional, and spiritual pain are passed onto our children because we have been emptied for so long, searching for other souls to fill voids that only we can fill. We use our sons and daughters to complete us, heal us, and fulfill us, turning them into our property by holding on to them and raising them for our own purpose instead of theirs. We've used them to take away our sadness, our broken hearts, but we forget that we've only been hurting them by transferring to them burdens, and traumas, that they've yet to understand. But by being aware of our dysfunctional habits, we can learn to do better and change those generational patterns.

Defeated Sons and Broken Daughters

As children, we are reflections of our parents, the people who raised us, and the people we see as our role models. We have our own minds, our own instincts, and we may not be exact replicas of our parents, but we innately model them in ways that most of us are unable to comprehend. In some ways, we act like them, we think like them, we behave like them, and at times subconsciously make similar decisions to theirs. I've sometimes caught myself saying things that my mother would say; it could be something as simple as "be careful," which she says whenever someone she cares for leaves home. I'm not always aware of when I say it, but I've picked it up from her because she's taught me to be a version of herself that has become a part of who I am.

We, as parents, often have the best intentions of raising our children right. We want them to be healthy, feel loved, have a bright future, and become something greater than we are. But wanting to give the best doesn't mean that we know how to give the best. It also doesn't mean that we have the best to give. According to data from the United States Census Bureau, more than 60 percent of African-descent children under the age of eighteen live in single-parent homes. This disproportionate statistic can create psychological wounds. Not to say single parents are not doing their best to raise their children to be well rounded and psychologically healthy individuals. This is definitely not meant to make any single parents feel as though they are incapable of doing an amazing job raising their sons and daughters. Just because you are, or were, raised in single-parent homes doesn't mean you're automatically broken. Growing up in a dysfunctional, toxic home with both parents can create more damage to a child psychologically than being raised in a healthy, loving single-parent home. But the truth is, you may not get the opportunity to experience a well-rounded upbringing that both parents were created to provide.

I am writing this as a son, a defeated son who has been loved by broken daughters. I am writing as a man, a fed-up man who has loved strong women. As sons, when we grow up watching our fathers—who do not measure up to the standards that our moms and society place on them—we feel like it's our responsibility to pick the slack, take care of things, and be the man that our dads should have been. Some of us step up and attempt to be the man that our mothers deserve, only to get defeated by our inability and unpreparedness to be men. We want to protect our mothers because our dads couldn't do it. We want to do whatever it takes to take care of our mothers because we understand that's what a man does. Many of us end up making premature decisions to grow up, skipping the stage of being a boy, because of the expectations that are placed on us or that we place on ourselves.

Defeated sons grow up rejecting the thought of becoming their fed-up fathers, only to end up being a different version of the man they hated. They grow up learning to take care of their mothers, only to grow up not knowing how to take care of and provide for their own partner and children. This is part of the negative cycle of not having a positive male role model.

As daughters, the cycle is not so different. When they see their moms take on every role in the household in a single or in a matriarchal dynamic, while being taught that it is a man's role to provide and protect, lead and love, the message becomes contradictory. The daughter starts formulating what she wants and doesn't want in a man. She starts designing herself in her mind and deciding who she will, and will not, be as a woman. She starts taking on her mother's pain, building her own resentments towards both Mom and Dad, trying to make sense of the clashing message between her biological intuition and her observations. As she deals with her own emotions, trying to be everything that society and her parents expect of her, she's learning to be strong by breaking down every virtue inside of her. Navigating the pressure of being a daughter, feeling rejected and neglected by the man who was supposed to be her first love, her chance to learn who she is, her purpose, and her self-worth starts weakening while her resilience and her threshold for pain becomes stronger and stronger. She feels disappointed in the woman who was supposed to model her biological feminine roles. She sees her mother in pain, taking on roles that shouldn't have been hers alone. She is equally disappointed in the man who should've been loving, masculine, and protective. Her pain continues when she meets a defeated boy who had to prematurely become a man. And so the cycle of defeat continues.

We love our sons and daughters. But until they heal from the traumas we as parents expose them to in their childhood, they'll treat their loved ones the same ways we treated them. As byproducts of slavery, we love our children the same way our masters loved us: with whips and violence. We love each other the same way our masters loved us: with shame and psychological abuse. We love our friends the same way our masters loved us: by calling each other derogatory names. We have become our masters to each other and to our children. Our sons and daughters learn our ways and teach their children those very same values and traditions.

CHAPTER 3

BROKEN DAUGHTERS

BEFORE I HAD A DAUGHTER, all I ever wanted was to experience the sweet, tender, loving affection of a sister. I wanted to play the big brother role, being protective and giving advice to my sister. Taking her out, buying her cute dresses, giving her all the princess treatments, making her feel special and pretty all the time. My vision of having a sister was to experience the feminine connection of a sweet little girl, who would grow up to become an emotionally mature, kind, caring, smart, loving woman. Little did I know my wish would be answered. I never knew paternal love, that deeply rooted love that would force you to let go of everything and live for that little person, until I had my daughter. As hard as it was for me to grasp the idea of not being in my child's life as a father, it became even harder for me to understand because I realized how much she needed me in her life and how much I needed her in mine. Every tiny little finger or toe hug showed me that my purpose in her life is to love her, to guide her, to protect her and to allow her to share every single part of my gifts: my mind, body, and soul, wholeheartedly. Whenever I placed her little body on my chest, it would feel like the world just stopped and we were the only ones living in it; we were frozen in time. That special bond I craved so much, that love I desired to share for so long, had finally come, and it has been some of the most precious days of my existence. To have that dear, honorable gift of being a father. To have been granted this responsibility of sharing this unwavering connection between a father and daughter. I could not have asked for anything greater, better, more precious—ever.

But with all that joy comes the responsibility to raise her to be mentally, emotionally, and physically whole. The decisions I make, the way I behave, what I want her to be accustomed to and find acceptable, depends on me. Who I am, as a man, a human being, a father, a partner, a son, a leader, a follower, will teach her about what, how, and who a man should aspire to be. I am her role model from now on. I possess the blueprint that will dictate some of her choices as she goes on through life. And so began my journey to be better. Not perfect, but better. Sometimes I may fall, other times, I will fail. I will make mistakes and screw up at times, because I am still human. But I've aspired to continuously be the healthiest version of myself, psychologically and physically, not just for my purpose, but for my daughter as well. For my loved ones. For me. And in that process, I realize how important having internal peace is and should be—again, not just for me but for everyone around me.

In order for me to share the healthiest version of myself, I needed to be at my healthiest. I needed to be healthy and whole if I wanted to pass on those attributes to her. Fathers, you don't have to be perfect. You don't have to be the best, the greatest, the richest, the fastest, because none of those things radiate perfection. Just strive to be purposeful and healthier daily: a healthier man, a healthier son, a healthier partner, a healthier friend, a healthier leader. Strive to be a healthier human being because your daughters are watching you. They deserve to feel loved and cherished by you. They deserve to feel wanted and protected by you. When they have doubts and questions about something as seemingly insignificant as their hair texture, they want to be reassured by you so they don't have to seek validation from boys and men who might only want to exploit them. You are Dad, their hero for as long as they feel loved, protected, and the most precious being in your eyes. It's your responsibility to heal yourself. It's your responsibility to teach her how a man loves. It won't always be easy, and it won't always be sweet. Sometimes I have to stay stern on my no with my four-year-old daughter and not give in when she tilts her head sideways and says, "Please, Daddy" when she asks for that third cupcake. You will become emotional when she tells you she's sad. Your daughters are counting on you to be there and be present for them. Remember, your strength is kindness, understanding, empathy, and humility; your masculinity is protection, guidance, and self-respect.

A Whole Life Ahead

As children, we all have a vision of how we would like our lives to be when we grow up. We have high expectations for ourselves and for what others expect of us. As a daughter, a sister, you didn't expect the world to be so hard on you. Dress this way, not that way, act this way if you want to be taken seriously. You're supposed to be nurturing, a caregiver, a healer, a helper, a mother, a daughter, a father, and even a son, because you feel obligated to meet every expectation that has been placed upon you. But has anyone noticed you? Has anyone seen the pain you have been given, have taken on, and are going through? Your first love may have disappointed you because he didn't understand your emotions. Because he became fed up and didn't know how to reach out to you. Your role model projected her pain onto you because she didn't want you to go through what she went through, but she never realized that she was only passing her baton to you so you can continue the fight. She's strong now. She has made it through her brokenness, she's trying to save you. But she broke you the day you saw her wiping her tears so you wouldn't notice that she was sad. She tries to show you her strength and hides her weaknesses because she's preparing you to be strong. But you're not ready. You haven't experienced your own pain yet. You haven't yet tried to fix somebody else's broken pieces while ignoring yours. You have been disappointed by your defeated, fed-up father who was never taught that he too needed to be healed; you shouldn't have to pay for his wounds. But you're learning. You're learning how to be resilient, strong, and capable. You're learning that your mother's life will never be your life, because you will be stronger. You're learning to take on it all by yourself because you were made for this. You were made for perfection. You're learning to neglect yourself to save those around you.

One day, those broken pieces you have yet to assemble will somehow fall into place because you're observing how to do it, although it hasn't worked for generations. You deserve to learn how to be kind, not hard; how to be caring not afraid. I get it: Mom and Dad were once broken and defeated, too. Their parents did the same thing to them. They want what's best for you, no question, but you can only give what you have. So, the hurt doesn't stop. Daddy couldn't be at your soccer practice because he had to work. He couldn't make it to your ballet recitals because he was taught that financial stability was way more important than mental stability. He needed to provide, he needed to protect. He's letting you down, and you try talking to him, but you don't feel the connection you're supposed to feel from a father. You become detached, heartbroken. Something inside of you leads you to find meaningless connections with boys and to try to fit in with friends who don't even like you. You put up with disrespectful and abusive behavior from others because you feel you deserve it. You feel you can fix it. You feel strong enough to not get broken. You're tired of having people walk out on you. You're drained from all the abuse you had to endure because of that emptiness, that void that refuses to be filled no matter how much you try.

My advice is to take your time, Princess. You didn't create the pain you're feeling, and that's why it's so hard for you to understand it. That's why nothing you've tried works. When you find yourself hurt and fragmented, your friends may tell you to move on and do what's best for you: live your best life and do what makes you happy. But as you keep searching and putting yourself in situations that break you down, take your time. Seek to understand the root of your pain. Don't blame others for it. It may have not been your fault, but it is your responsibility to find healing. It is your responsibility to learn how much you have to give before your cup runs empty. No one can heal your pain or fill the void but you. Before you choose to continue to go down that broken, self-destructive path, find the healing that you need. Consider the role models you had growing up and the blueprint they gave you to follow. Seek to understand the roots of your pain and confusion.

External Beauty

I was reading Former President Barack Obama's book *Of Thee I Sing: A Letter to My Daughters* to my four-year-old daughter one day. It had illustrations of kids and adults. One of them was a picture of a little European-descent girl in a blue dress with long straight hair tied in a ponytail. While I was reading, my daughter pointed at the picture and said, "I want to look like this girl." I didn't think anything of it at first, but it sparked my curiosity, so I asked her, "Why do you want to look like her, my love?" She said, "Because she is beautiful; she has long pretty hair and she has a pretty princess dress on." That answer made my heart skip a beat. I said, "She is beautiful, but what about this girl in the yellow dress?" pointing to a little African-descent girl with short, natural hair. She told me that the girl didn't look like a princess because princesses have long hair and look like the girl in the blue dress. I said, "But that girl in the yellow dress looks like you and you are a princess!"

As the conversation continued, I repeated that she was as pretty as the girl with the long hair and reminded her that she also had pretty dresses. But my daughter insisted that she didn't look like a princess because her hair wasn't long and didn't look like that little girl in the book. I tried to convince her that she was beautiful just the way she looks, and that her short, natural hair was beautiful just like Mommy's, and she was my beautiful princess, something that she had heard from me and her mom countless times. But that nagging image in the back of her mind about the definition of Western beauty had already tainted her self-worth. I was brokenhearted to learn that my own daughter was becoming a victim of society's characterization of female beauty. As much as her mother and I have tried to instill confidence in her by teaching her to possess self-love, self-assurance, kindness, intelligence, creativity—and other attributes that make a well-rounded, good person—television, movies, and the Internet expose our kids to different examples of what it means to be beautiful. It's no coincidence that, until recently, the Disney princesses were all of European descent.

For many African-descent girls and women, the idea of beauty comes from the images portrayed by Western cultures. This includes having flawless light skin; long, wavy hair; long, slim legs; and symmetrical facial features. It's no wonder they feel that way. I have heard African-descent men say, "She's fine, light skin, slim, with the right size derriere and long curly hair." Are we still so attached to the slave mentality that our own image becomes a symbol of ugliness to ourselves? We live in a culture that teaches young girls that their external beauty is more important than who they are on the inside. We use external physical features to bully, classify, and define humanity. As parents raising daughters, and even sons, our job becomes harder and harder because we are fighting the external forces of every media outlet, every princess movie, every idealized doll as a point of reference to define how we should look. I've seen young girls grow up thinking that they are defined by their physical appearance, and they use it as a means to get what they want or allow boys to use it against them to get what *they* (the boys) want. Their perceived notion of beauty becomes their weakness. They're fixated on hearing reassurances about how pretty and sexy they are, and they feel empty and unloved if they don't get that. So many smart little girls miss out on their true purpose because they waste their teenage years chasing their physical beauty by attracting anyone who will provide them with validation.

Women waste a lifetime of emotional gifts on bad relationships with men who use their yearning for constant beauty reminders. How do we get past this? The idea that my daughter and so many other little brown skin girls may become victims of Western definitions of beauty truly breaks my heart. I want her to feel smart. I want her to feel valued, loved, purposeful, belonged, and beautiful. I want her to make a positive impact in others' lives by making a difference, using her internal beauty, her kindness, and by being a virtuous woman. I want her to create and build up her generation and the next. I want her to know that her body and soul are beautiful, and all she needs to do is take care of that gift, that temple, that castle she was born in. I want her to know and feel that external validation is not compulsory but, rather, appreciated. I want her to value every gift that she was born with and appreciate them. Her skin complexion, her nose, her lips, her eyes, her ears, her hair, her body—it's all a gift and it's the perfect one. I want her to know that she should never let anyone take away that gift from her. I want her to know that no one can make that gift look better or feel better; she is the sole owner of that gift and it's her responsibility to take good care of it, protect it, and be discerning with whom she chooses to share her gift.

Unsung Beauty

As a man, I've made some decisions in my life based on how I've been told I look. I've been told "you can do this" because I have a certain kind of look. But I'll tell you honestly, none of that advice or flattery ever got me to my purpose. Being told I was smart, *believing* I was smart, got me seeing things differently. Your purpose has nothing to do with how you look. Your destiny has nothing to do with your physical features and the materialistic things you attach yourself to. We've been brought up to believe these things are paramount, because we live in a society that is obsessed with external attributes.

Doing the right thing has nothing to do with the color of your skin or your body shape or your ethnic background. Being a good human being has nothing to do with how long your hair is or how pretty your dress looks. Being of service to those in need has nothing to do with how flat or pointy your nose is, or how thick or thin your thighs are. Being a healer has nothing to do with how tall or short you are. It has nothing to do with how big or small you are. Being kind has nothing to do with where you came from or how rich or poor your family may be. Being smart doesn't care if you drive a luxury car or if you live in a mansion or in a shack. You can't buy or sell internal attributes, but you can promote them. You can encourage your daughters to be confident and kind. Young girls can learn to see themselves as smart and caring instead of pretty and sexy. It starts with understanding that they were born beautiful and that nothing about them is a mistake that needs improvement. Little girls, like my daughter, can start rejecting the notion that long hair and princess dresses make them pretty. Young girls can stop expecting physical gratification from external sources and letting young boys and degenerate men use them for their sexual satisfaction. When young girls recognize their self-worth, when they start focusing on their internal beauty instead of their external appearance, they'll develop greater emotional stability and establish healthier relationships.

Accountability

One thing our culture doesn't do is teach our young girls to take accountability for themselves and their actions. This includes how to be physically strong and defend themselves when need be, how to make wise decisions, and how to be responsible for their bodies, their health, their values, their morals, and their lives.

For a young girl, taking accountability means that she is in control of her behavior because she's aware of the consequences. She understands the fact that no one else values her life and her safety more than she does. We live in a beautiful world that produces some mentally unwell human beings, disturbed souls searching for others to hurt and take advantage of. I don't mean to say that there is darkness in everyone, but not everyone has your best interests at heart. As a young girl, you will meet great people, make great friends, fall in love, fall out of love, and even get your heart broken. Always remember you have the power to select whom you choose to share your gift with. No one is entitled to your gift and no one has the right to take your gift away from you. Whether you fail or succeed, fall or thrive, taking accountability for you and your actions only makes you a better person. You can learn from mistakes that were made whether you were at fault or not, because it is your responsibility to extract the lessons. Embrace your slipups as your own; learn to use them to grow and become better. Even though not every failure is your fault, it will always be your responsibility to heal from them whenever they affect you mentally, emotionally, and spiritually.

Being accountable for what you do, where you go, and whom you're with will also help you understand that you have no control over what other people do or how they choose to act towards you, but you owe it to yourself to choose to be surrounded with kindness, efficiency, positivity, and love. Everyone should be held accountable for his or her actions. And if, God forbid, you ever become the victim of something through no fault of your own, don't let it become the worst of you. Even if there was nothing you could have done differently, learn from it, and allow it to help you grow and become a better version of yourself. Don't be afraid to take accountability for your emotions and feelings, positive or negative. Admitting you're wrong, when you are, doesn't make you a weak or a bad person. You are responsible for how you act and react to situations that are in your control. Own that. People will test you, your patience, and your kindness; life will be tough at times, and your emotions will dictate how you respond to provocations. But remember, you can't control what others say or do and how they say or do it—but you do have the ability to control how you let it affect you mentally, psychologically, and spiritually. And you can also control whether you choose to remain in that environment or not.

The Princess Syndrome

As a father to a loving daughter, I always want to be able to give her what she wants, especially when she makes that cute half-smiley, half-pouty face. It's so hard to resist, but it's necessary. We need to teach our children, and ourselves, the difference between our wants and needs, so that they don't ask for what we can't afford. We must teach them, and ourselves, that material things bring no value to our lives. There's absolutely nothing wrong with making your children feel loved and happy by giving them something they've always wanted and deserved. But the problem arises when parents don't know how to love their children because of their own emptiness, so they buy their hearts and affection with material things whether they can afford it or not. They are afraid to say no to their children because they fear they're going to lose their love and approval. Or perhaps they don't have time to be with their children or even lack emotional empathy. So they use gifts and or money out of guilt or to avoid having any emotional interaction with their children. When this happens, girls can grow up to feel entitled and self-centered because they've always gotten what they wanted—on demand. They never learn to differentiate their wants versus their needs. I call this the "Princess Syndrome." A girl with princess syndrome will throw tantrums if she doesn't get what she wants immediately. She'll be hard to please as an adult because her appetite for receiving has become insatiable. This syndrome will create an emotional void that she won't know how to fill because the real, nonmaterialistic love she needed as a child was never given to her.

As parents, it's our responsibility to provide our children love, affection, and attention. Society teaches us to prioritize what we want over what we need because capitalism thrives when we buy, buy, buy. Our children grow up empty and unsatisfied because their real, emotional needs are never met. Parents should know the difference between wants and needs, teach their children to understand the difference, and make this conscious awareness a part of everyday life.

Needing Your Parents

When we buy something that needs to be assembled, it usually comes with a manual and instructions on how to care for the product. As children, our parents are that manual. And if they are believers, the Bible can also be used as a manual, alongside grandparents and other respected, trusted family members, to guide, raise, and teach morals, values, and traditions. Sadly, in our culture it's rare for our children to get the combined manual and directions of both parents. As daughters, you need your parents as much as they need you. You need your mother to teach you about womanhood, how to navigate being a girl and a young woman in a culture that every so often will confuse you with all its options and teachings. You need your mother to teach you values to live by when friends are pressuring you to do something you know you shouldn't do. You need her to reinforce your confidence when you feel as if being who you are and what you were taught are being compromised. Your mother is your manual; she's seen and had her share of some of the things you are experiencing. As the saying goes, "There's nothing new under the sun"—believe it. The expressions may be different, the messengers may look different, the experiences may feel different; but don't cast her out because you feel like she won't or doesn't understand your experiences. She wants what's best for you more than friends do, more than boys do, more than society does. If you spend time understanding her—her ways, her habits, her pain, her mistakes, her triumphs—you will understand yourself more than you know. So read and understand that manual. Some instructions you won't find useful in terms of behavior; some you won't understand in terms of experiences; some will be irrelevant in comparison to your own. But for the most part, you have her for a reason: you need her.

One thing that breaks my spirit as an African-descent father is the lack of recognition and importance our culture places on African-descent men as fathers. Whether we as fathers are to blame for not taking care of our responsibilities and assuming active roles in raising our children or whether it's the mothers who claim the children are theirs and disqualify us as fathers, doesn't matter. The fact is, none of those reasons benefit our children. As a father to a little girl who will grow up to have interactions with boys and men, it's essential that I am a part of her life. Whether her mother and I are together or not, I'm still responsible; and it is my godly and innate duty to provide my part of that manual that she needs in order to fully become who she was intended and created to be.

So daughters, I appeal this to you: your relationship with your father is potentially a reflection of the relationship you will share with someone of the opposite sex. I understand that it is not, and should not, be your responsibility to create that relationship with your father, especially if he's not in your life. But, as a young father to a little girl, I understand the importance of having him in your life. You might only hear negative things about your father and we, fathers and African-descent men, must accept responsibility if and when we caused these negative feelings.

We must learn to raise sons who will be responsible and good men, protective and kind men. Men who are healthy enough to love their daughters, not with their pain and shortcomings, but with honesty, respect, grit, understanding, wisdom, kindness, and empathy. I hope we, as fathers, are open to learning how to love and care for our daughters beyond the destructive and unhealthy patriarchal ways that we were taught. Our daughters need us, they deserve to have us in their lives—so let's make a conscious effort to not rob them of that part of the manual, that love and bond that we were created to share with them.

CHAPTER 4

STRONG WOMEN: YOUR STRENGTH

I'VE HAD DISCUSSIONS WITH SELF-STYLED strong independent African-descent women. While there's absolutely nothing wrong with possessing strength, resilience, and kindness, referring to oneself as a strong person can negatively impact how others see and treat you, as well as how you see and treat others. Sometimes when we become strong emotionally, we are not that way by choice; strength can come from generational suffering or by bearing the responsibility of our negative experiences. During slavery, the African-descent woman was expected to be strong and capable of bearing anything. She was seen as emotionally and physically strong because she wasn't seen as a normal human being. To go through everything our ancestors went through, and still manage to rise, fight, escape, protest, and make it out to where we are today, takes a superhuman. As byproducts of slavery, we were left with everything that was expected of our ancestors, as well as everything that was taught to them.

Growing up in the Caribbean, I used to hear my grandmother asking God for strength in order to deal with her calamities. Whenever she would have an ache or she was stressed or sad, she would plead, "Bondye banm fos" (God give me strength). As a child, listening to her asking God for strength would always make me feel sad, because I knew she was in pain; she was hurting more than she could ever express and I couldn't do anything to help her. I never quite understood how acquiring strength would help take away or heal her pain. She would pray day and night, sing hymns and old Negro spirituals, but her pain would never end. I've come to realize that we don't need strengthening, we need healing. We don't need fighting spirits to fight our battles; we need understanding in order to determine where our wounds came from, what's causing them, and how to heal from them. Because when God saves you and gives you strength, you will always need to ask him to save you or to give you strength. Only when you're healed will you be able to let go of the anger, hurt, pain, resentment, disappointment, trauma, and brokenness and start valuing yourself, your peace of mind, and everything that brings you joy and moves you closer to your life's purpose. Unfortunately, I still hear mothers and daughters praying and crying for strength to get through hard times. Every Sunday at church, we pray for those who persecute us, hate on us, bring us pain—but we always fail to look at ourselves, our traditions, our cultures, and our own detrimental habits. We fail to pay attention and understand the patterns our parents and grandparents passed down to us. To the African-descent woman, emotional strength has been a tradition since slavery, because there was no healing for our ancestors' never-ending miseries. It wasn't easy for them to be optimistic that better days were ahead. They were forced to believe, because of their strength, hope, and faith in the Lord, that there would be a better place waiting for them after enduring their endless agonies. Throughout history, African-descent women have always been the symbol of strength.

Watching your children getting ripped out of your hands due to gun violence destroyed you. Feeling like the welfare system made you have to choose between your children and the man you may have loved, gave you few options. As I mentioned before, there's absolutely nothing wrong with being a strong person mentally, emotionally, and physically. But understand that you don't always *have* to be strong and it's okay to allow yourself to be vulnerable, humble, accountable, and, most importantly, healed.

The Unspoken Expectations

As African-descent children in our culture, our boys and girls are forced to evolve psychologically before they can even have a sense of who they are. They are involuntarily enduring ancestral and familial detriments at an alarming rate, and the saddest part is that our culture is cheering for them. I watched a video recently during one of the Black Lives Matter protests after one of our brothers was murdered by a police officer. This little girl, who couldn't have been any older than five or six, was holding a sign that read "no justice, no peace" while marching and protesting, with power and might, angry and fed up with racism and racial injustice like everyone else. She was cheered on by our people. They were cheering because they saw this fire in her to fight for justice and equality. They were cheering for the power she demonstrated with her fist and her shouts amidst the other protesters' cries for justice and the police response of automatic weapons and tear gas. She was already strong enough to fight a battle that she shouldn't have to fight at such a young age, but we encouraged it.

What kind of childhood are we giving our children if we're cheering for them to fight battles that they can't even yet comprehend? Are we directly and indirectly, consciously and subconsciously, teaching our children to adapt to our brokenness and detrimental ways when we should be protecting them, loving on them, and giving them the necessary tools they need to be emotionally, spiritually, and physically healthy? Putting our children in situations to fight our battles, when they don't even understand who they are themselves, doesn't help them; it hurts them.

As African-descent women, you are seen as having all these strengths. Strong reactions, strong expressions, strong opinions, strong minds, strong wills—you walk around tough as nails, which oftentimes may be perceived as angry and aggressive even when you're not. You have a lot of passion. You have a lot of hurt because of all the trauma you have had to carry with you. Your friends see you as a strong woman, because they need you to be strong so they can be strong. Your children see you as a strong woman, because you're doing everything to make sure they have what they need and are taken care of. Your family sees you as a strong woman, because you have a fight in you and you never back down. When others are hurting and need someone, you're the strong one they call on. But when you're hurting, you need someone; you hang on to your pain. Friends will tell you you're strong just so they don't have to deal with your pain. Having strength will come in handy, but it won't help you heal. Praying for healing, seeking help, trying to understand the source of your trauma and dealing with it so you don't have to constantly use strength to fuel your journey, are healthy actions.

Oftentimes in our culture, when someone faces a tragedy, such as the loss of a loved one or a failed relationship, we tell him or her that "you are strong, you can get through this, and if anyone can endure it, it is you." But having the ability to cope with trauma has nothing to do with how strong or weak one is. Being able to regain joy and some type of normalcy after a loss has nothing to do with being strong; if that were the case, most of us would be in constant grief from our daily struggles. It is contingent upon your support system, how mentally healthy you are in the way you process experiences, and how much resilience you have built when it comes to adversity, pain, hurt, brokenness, and dysfunction. We have become accustomed to enduring pain, disappointments, and generational hurt. Our ability to either cope with or crumble from a despairing situation is far greater than others'.

Being a strong woman allows you to hold on to your hurt, your burdens, and every cross you have to bear because if you don't, no one else will. You were expected to tolerate all that you have been put through—so you've built up enough invulnerability to the things that could have destroyed you, had you not been through the traumatic experiences over and over again.

The odds against you have been unforgivable. The disparity of medical care, the enormous gap of mental health accessibility in our communities, the unfair disproportion of raising children on your own, and watching your sons and daughters getting ripped right out of your arms. No wonder you have developed the strength to endure. It's the one thing that has kept you going when you felt like the world was against you; it's the one thing that has kept you going when you have had nowhere and no one to turn to. It's that strength that has been keeping you going when it all seems too much to bear.

But that strength has also kept you shattered, hurt, and in agony. That strength that you've come to rely on in our communities has also prevented you from healing. Relying upon your strength to get you through adversity means not understanding the source of your pain and allowing yourself to heal. It means finding yourself in situations that require you to use your strength and becoming even more vulnerable to hurt. It means responding to circumstances using your strength, because it's the one thing that has gotten you through the tough times. Using your strength as a resource to live life is exhausting and will take a toll on your mental health and those closest to you.

Holding On to Who You Are

In some of my past relationships, women would say, "Love me for who I am, and either you take me or leave me." As someone who has always been conscious of being a healthier version of myself, the idea of loving someone for who they are would oftentimes scare me. Although I do accept and love every human being wholeheartedly, this would raise some red flags. For one, this woman is not open to change. Second, she's not open to being a healthier person, whether psychologically or physically. Third, she's not coachable and not teachable. Fourth, what happens when I change and become healthier—will she accept my changes? Fifth, she's more comfortable holding onto her learned pain and brokenness, and is not consciously willing to heal and become greater. Just like today is not quite like yesterday, we are all subject to change. Our moods change, our energy levels change, our minds change, our emotions change, and our interests change from time to time. We are changing daily, unless you're the kind of person who is done growing.

It's ironic how so many of us, even in our adulthood, are still hanging on for dear life to every single bad habit our parents taught us. We refuse to let those detrimental behaviors go, even if they're clearly destroying everything we want to be and want to build into our lives. We hold on to every negative thing we were taught like a badge of honor, because we don't want to disappoint or hurt our role models. We hang onto these negative habits out of loyalty, and somehow we fail to acknowledge that they were broken too. Asking someone to love you for who you are limits the level of love you could actually be receiving. You're essentially putting a cap on yourself and expecting to be who you are for as long as you're with that person. The moment you attempt to grow or show change, that person will be sure to remind you that you've changed and may no longer be interested in who you're becoming. You could have avoided months, years, or even a lifetime of hurt, disappointment, and pain.

Being open to change is scary, I get it—but not being loved for the person you should aspire to be is even scarier. Our parents taught us to be who we are and who we should be. Some of us had great parents who provided for us and loved us the best way they knew how. But we also have to understand that they taught us what they knew, how they knew it, and why we should know it. The sooner you understand who you are, the more likely it is that you will become who you were meant to be. You'll be able to let go of the notion of who you were and start walking in your purpose.

The idea of seeing yourself as you already are, with no need on your part to grow or change, can be detrimental to relationships, whether it's with friends, family or a mate. Even though we should accept everyone for who they are, someone you want to build a future with should also be loved for the person they intend to become; this includes accepting their vision, and seeing yourself as part of that vision.

Loving You and Being Loved by You

The most powerful love a man can ever experience, next to God, is the love of a generous, caring, and emotionally healthy woman. Your passion, your kindness, your gentle ways can make us feel powerful, manly, successful, and productive. The way you have our back can make us feel like we have reached the epitome of manhood. The way you know the things to say when it matters most. The way you make us feel, when you proudly look at us and see every fiber of our being, can create a bond so deep, so pure, that you can tell when we're sad just by the sound of our voice. A hug, a touch on the shoulder, a simple reassurance that everything is going to be all right, can give us everlasting hope and strengthen our faith in the unimaginable. The way you pray for us and cheer for us makes us feel safe and makes the impossible feel possible.

For some of us, it starts with our mothers who gave up everything to give us everything they had. You selflessly commit to keeping us safe, protected, fed, cleaned, supported, and loved. In spite of your own pain, your own brokenness, you've devoted your entire life to give us life. For others, it may start with a grandmother, friend, a spouse, a sister, or even a cousin.

Majestic woman, the depth of your love goes deeper than what you were given from slavery. It goes back to when the sun that kissed your skin in the African valleys gave you your golden complexion and passionate ways. How did we get here? The aches of your soul shadow your love at times; and with that love you give, we feel every part of your agony. We kings want to protect you, love you, cherish you, and go with you towards your purpose, but a lot of us don't know how. We are not being taught how to be what you want us to be; and the love we receive from you sometimes leaves us in pain and broken, just like you are in pain and broken. Still, we leave you to carry the burdens on your own, with all your tears and sorrows. As beautiful as being loved by you and loving you could and should be, our mutual brokenness robs us of our future and peace with each other.

Society has created ways to hurt you and put you down, and when you muster the courage to raise children on your own, the last thing African-decent men should do is bring you more pain and more sadness. We have hurt you by giving up on you instead of seeking to understand you. Believing that you're always right, instead of challenging you to be healthier, gives us the excuse to be absent, silent, and live in your shadow while you take on the roles that we, as men, partners, and fathers, were meant to take on. We have used that belief to act irresponsibly because we know you got it. But I have faith in us. I have confidence that we will find healing and love each other in ways that bring about change in our communities, our lives, and our children, and to our countries.

Your Emotionally Wounded Girlfriends

I believe each and every one of us has these three types of friends. One is the type of friend who means well and wants everything glorious for you. They help you grow, prosper, and heal, and fuel your path towards your purpose. Others are those who are intentionally wicked and are cheering for your downfall. They pretend to like you while they drag you down behind your back. Lastly, there are those who are just there to cheer you on and validate every decision you make, even if it is detrimental for your well-being and purpose. The path they're on is all they know, and it's all they have to offer to you.

The fact is, none of us were meant to do this life journey alone. We need family, we need friends, we need meaningful connections, we need each other. But in times when you need to heal, when you need to understand yourself, and when you need to become healthier and live a purposeful life, the most damaging friends are the ones who are hurting, broken, and living vicariously through your vulnerability. Those are the friends who are there to encourage you to live your best life when you are at your lowest point. The friends who encourage you to do what makes you happy, when everything that may seem to make you happy only brings more destruction to your path. They know the right things to say to validate your pain, but they are not able to lead you to a healing or healthier path. I'm not saying a friend who is hurting can't understand your pain and help you work through it—but until they understand and acknowledge their own pain, they won't be capable of helping you with yours.

Sometimes when we are hurting because we have lost someone who meant everything to us, whether through our fault or not, we may be angry, sad, and confused. We may want justice and revenge. And a friend who is hurting, who no longer has anything to lose, can help you lose everything by uplifting you to choose destructive paths. Furthermore, if those friends are envious of what you have and think your pain is not as great as theirs, they will encourage you to make irrational and unproductive decisions. Be mindful of whom you share your pain with and whom you bring into your emptiness. Not every friend is the same, and not every friend shares your purpose and intention.

Raising Your Sons

As a son who at some point grew up with a single mother and not knowing his biological father, I remember feeling unwanted even when I didn't have reasons to feel that way. I felt unwanted because my brothers had their father, some of my cousins had their fathers, some of my friends had their fathers, but I didn't. Having had the foundation that my grandparents instilled in me, I would always depend on their love, their attention, when I felt bereft. Raising a child as a single parent is hard for both mother and child. It's not always the case that a mother is unfit to raise that child by herself, but she is often unable to understand and teach that child everything he or she was meant to be taught and experienced by both parents. As a mother to a son, the way you treat him will affect how he's treated in his future sentimental relationships. His perception of you will dictate how he views women in the future. He will either detest how you treated him and avoid committing to a woman at all costs, or he will find and create a similar relationship paradigm.

I know that mothers who are raising their sons on their own have to provide, protect, teach, and discipline. It is not easy. But your primary responsibility to your sons is to nurture and love them in ways that only a woman and a mother can. You can't love your sons for their fathers and you can't make up for their fathers' absences. It may be a hard pill to swallow, but teaching your sons what their fathers are supposed to teach them shouldn't be your responsibility. Your job is to teach them how a woman should behave towards a son, a boy, and a man—and, if there is no man in the house, how a son, boy, or man should treat a woman by how you accept being treated by the men around you. Your job is to love him and teach him how to accept and appreciate the essence of a woman. You teach him what an emotionally, physically, and spiritually healthy woman is and should be, so he knows what he should aim to find one day. Show him what a healthy woman does—show him how she loves herself and those closest to her, how she appreciates herself, and how she should carry herself.

Biologically, every child has a sense of what his or her natural behaviors and adaptations should be; but his or her upbringing will greatly influence those natural senses. That upbringing includes the child's culture, tradition, and faith-based beliefs, among other factors. If you want to raise emotionally healthy boys who will become well-rounded and emotionally healthy men, you first have to be emotionally healthy yourself. Your sons need you to love them as a woman and a mother; be patient with them, be kind to them. The truth is, your sons need their fathers just as much as they need you. Teaching your sons how *not* to be like their fathers out of bitterness and anger creates a psychological burden. And a single mom's mentality doesn't only apply to single moms. Mothers can still be in a relationship and have a single mom's mentality. When you have disagreements with your spouse or partner, and the kids become your weapon to get what you want, you are destroying them psychologically. The way you treat the men in your life will be your sons' perceptions of how women treat men and how they should deal with them. It's important to be the woman you want them to attract, and it's up to you to model that for them.

It's safe to say that most African-descent men are being raised, or have been raised, by their mothers. And sometimes the mothers have been hurt, disappointed, and broken but are still trying to give their children the best they can. This is not to say that having a defeated and fed-up father would make this relationship better. But raising your sons by trying to take their father's ways out of them and teaching them how to be men who won't hurt women, when you yourself are hurting, will not necessarily teach them how to be emotionally healthy men. Not having an early emotionally and psychologically healthy male in their lives will not only hurt them long term, but it will be a recipe for hurting our daughters when they get older. Also, when they see their mother hurting and in pain, they won't know what a content, wholesome, kind, sweet, tender, patient woman is supposed to be like; they will eventually settle for what they are familiar with—another you.

If your son thinks you're crazy as a mother, he will think that most women are crazy. If you are angry and aggressive, he will have learned that African-descent women are angry and aggressive. You are his point of reference, his first impression of a woman. Are you proud of that woman? And if he detests your ways and goes against everything you were to him, he'll be confused and emotionally damaged, which is a recipe for hurt and brokenness.

Raising Your Daughters

My daughter loves her mom. It's such a beautiful sight watching them being joyful and playful together. She looks up to her mother, she imitates her, models her. Isn't it awesome to know that your daughters will one day be women and may potentially be like you, her mother? Your character, your behavior, your demeanor; the way you speak, act, treat others, love yourself, love others; your kindness, your meanness, your habits—all of it. Or will she dislike your ways so much so that she swears to never be like you? As a mother to daughters, you are looking at the next generation of yourself. What are you passing down to them? Are you building emotionally healthy and stable women for the future? Are you building kind, caring, nurturing foundations they'll be able to build on and pass down to the next generation of children and grandchildren? Are you showing them what kind of romantic partners they'll need to choose to share their hearts, bodies, and purpose with? Your choices as a mother to your daughters matter because they are watching your every move. They see you as their role model. They see themselves in your eyes.

The way you treat and love yourself will determine how they love and treat themselves. You have the power to create the best possible version of yourself. When you envision that version of yourself, what do you see? Do you see somebody strong, hurt, broken, anxious, depressed, prideful, unkind, loud, selfish, obnoxious, unhealthy, unloved, stressed, afraid, insensitive, uneducated, unteachable, and with low self-esteem? Or do you see somebody kind, loving, self-sufficient, smart, confident, loving, humble, gracious, accountable, peaceful, generous, giving, beautiful inside and out? Don't teach them how not to be like you. Create a life that you are proud of, a life that you want to pass down to them and that they can pass down as generational blessings to their own children and future generations. Only you can love them like a mother can. Their fathers will love them like you love your son, but never as you love them. Embrace that privilege. Use that power to create physically, emotionally, and spiritually healthy girls and women.

Your Honesty

As mothers, are you honest with your children? I understand it's not easy and may not even be a question, because you are the hero. But, if nothing else, be honest with your daughters. They'll carry your honesty into their relationships, and they'll make decisions based on your truths. Be honest with your sons, because they love you and they'll do anything to protect you. Don't let them base that love on the false pretense that you've never done wrong or you were the victim of your circumstances. I've seen so many adults making hurtful decisions based on a one-sided story from one parent. They'll see one parent as the rogue and the other as the hero. It's neither healthy nor helpful to the children, and you're hurting and scarring those children for the rest of their lives. It's unfair and it's cruel. One of the unhealthiest things you can do for your sons and daughters is to let them draw their own conclusions of what may have gone wrong between you and your partner.

Your Relationship Patterns

I was recently part of a panel discussing fatherhood and what is lacking in our communities. It's unfortunate that so many children end up being raised by parents who make those children their own pet projects. In that discussion, there was a young woman who insisted on how strong she was and needed to be as a woman, because she would never let a man control her. This raised several issues. The need to protect yourself from men who are not even in your life can be a huge detriment to your psychological health and any future relationships. If you feel like this woman, you are walking around guarded and in defense mode, preparing yourself to not get hurt when, in fact, you are hurting yourself daily. As I wrote earlier, strength is holding you back from experiencing life and love. As the saying goes, hurt people hurt people. If you are getting into relationships and consciously loving people with your strength, you are basically creating broken and painful relationships that will bring you nothing but hurt and pain in return.

We, as a people, need to understand what makes us strong. Kindness makes you strong. Being loving, empathetic, and slow to anger make you strong. It takes a second to destroy someone, but it takes a lifetime to build somebody up; that's strength. It takes courage to seek healing and become healthier; wallowing in your pain, guarding yourself from hurt that may come, holding onto past traumas because it gives us an excuse to justify our anger and resentments, are not acts of strengths. Anything that destroys you physically, emotionally, spiritually, and psychologically is not strength.

One of the questions that the young woman on the panel asked me was, "Have you ever been a woman?" I didn't answer, because the question was obviously rhetorical. Time and time again, I've heard women say, "We're tired of raising and building grown men." I can imagine that's got to be exhausting. I've also heard women say, "Before I can allow a man to lead, I need to make sure he's a good leader." To this I say we are all leaders and we are all followers. But most of us don't know how to play those roles, partly because some of us never witnessed those roles being performed, at least not in a healthy and constructive way. I understand how women can be tired of raising half-raised men, because men are also tired of fighting with half-raised women. Men are also exhausted having to prove to women, who never witnessed healthy leadership from their fathers, telling them how to be leaders. It didn't work coming from their mother, it won't work coming from you, his woman. But we'll get to the men in Chapter Six and more detail about leadership later on in this chapter.

We often go into relationships with our perceptions all twisted and wrong. If your view of your father was shaped by what you saw as a child, which may have been how an absent or terrible father treated your mother, you won't have the best perception of men.

What steps have you taken in order to heal your broken views before you start seeing another man? When did you start getting rid of those unwanted characteristics in your father before projecting them on your partner? A lot of us grew up in households with parents displaying relationships we say we'd never have when we grow up, but unfortunately we end up having similar or worse relationship experiences than what we grew up witnessing. You try to avoid being in their shoes, but you've never worked through, and healed from, those traumas. In life, whatever you place a magnifying glass on is what you see more clearly; and the longer you focus on those negative characteristics, the worst they'll become. If you learned how a woman treats a man from your mother, ask yourself if she was the best example for you in that arena.

Don't look at your mother as a mother; look at her as a woman, a wife, a partner. Is that who you want to be in order to have the relationship you want? When did you get rid of your mother's negative views of men that ended up shaping your views? It's unfortunate that as boys and girls we already have damaging emotional experiences with the opposite sex before even getting in a relationship. We go into relationships with preconceived ideas of what we should expect based on what we lived through and experienced from watching and listening to our parents. The key is to release those negative and unhealthy habits we were given by our parents, and find healing, healthy, and purposeful ways that will benefit our relationships and those of future generations.

Acquiring and Accepting Help

None of us was created to do this life journey alone. We are conditioned to fool ourselves into thinking that we don't need a man or woman, but the fact is, we do. Again, I think a lot of us are confusing our needs with our wants. We have been taught to value our wants more than our needs because most of our wants are attainable by hard work, monetary status, and power. We can control our wants with strength and might, and that makes us feel less vulnerable and coldhearted at the same time. Our dominance over our wants makes us feel in control because they are ours. We purchase them, we own them, we can discard them at any time and in any way we see fit. We devalue anyone we can't control—anyone who won't do what we want, how we want, and when we want. There's a danger in that. We can convince ourselves we have super strength and super power and can do anything all by ourselves, and it will be done right, just the way only we can do it, the best way. But at what expense? As independent as you may feel, we have each other for a purpose. Don't let your perfectionism create a world of loneliness like a self-sustained island. You may have been let down and disappointed in ways that no one but you may ever understand, but if you try to do everything your way and only the way you want, it may cost you your peace of mind, your mental health and stability, and even your relationships.

A few things happen when you cast off or depreciate others' help; for one, you lose resources and put more pressure on yourself. Two, you are creating your own world of rejection and isolation. Three, you will make others believe that you can handle things all by yourself, even if it kills you. But you are creating and choosing an unhealthy path. Maybe it's your spouse or a partner, family members and friends, but understand that perfection is an illusion created to make you feel in control and better than. Not everything needs to be "perfect," at least not in the way you would want. Is it worth your peace of mind if the bed is not made perfectly, or the food doesn't taste as good as you would have made it, or the kids are not cared for the way you would have cared for them? Sometimes it's best to value others' spirit of giving when they want to make our lives easier by helping us carry our daily load. Appreciate their willingness to create other paths for us to walk on and help us maintain our emotional health and peace of mind. Shifting our minds to value good friends and loved ones will help us recognize good people instead of those who just say and do things that make us feel good when it benefits them, even when those people are not good for us.

Don't Delegate—Teammate

John Donne said it best when he wrote, "No man is an island." But how do you create a teammate relationship when you've never been part of a team? If you grow up watching your parents and siblings putting their own best interests first and doing what serves them, you will learn to be your own team and the captain of your own ship and do what's best for you. We sometimes fail in relationships and parenting because we adopt that same "I'm doing what's best for me" mentality. Creating a teammate-driven relationship is not about doing what's best for me, but rather what's best for us. It's not about delegating and telling everyone what to do, when to do it, and how to do it, because at some point that will only create frustration, resentment, chaos, and exhaustion. When you create a teammate-approach relationship, you know that when one player fails, it affects the team. With this mindset, the willingness to win together will surpass any self-serving and self-protecting attitude.

Approaching any relationship with the delegate attitude prevents and discourages the other players from learning, participating, growing, and contributing to the team. If a team is a one-player-driven entity, that team will suffer and subsequently crumble. In order to have a team that serves and benefits the unit, one cannot perceive himself or herself as the only one playing to win. The team must set forth strategies that work for every player and each player must understand his or her role and what that role entails. A plan to triumph as a team must be established; otherwise, the stability and the potential of that team will diminish.

Leaders and Followers

As mentioned earlier, when I hear women say their man is not a good leader and they can't follow him, I ask, "Are you a follower? Who taught you what leadership was?" When many of us think of bad leadership and following, we envision being put on a leash and getting dragged into a brick wall. We perceive good leadership as having someone who will do everything according to our perceptions and viewpoints, who will protect us at all costs and always make the right decisions. Our definition and perception of leading and following is defined by our lingering fear of slavery and being hurt, which is what we observed and learned from our parents' broken relationships and damaging past experiences.

The truth is, many women and girls in our communities weren't raised in ways that facilitate that kind of relationship paradigm. If you were raised by your mother, whether single or with a single mom mentality, you weren't raised to follow a man. Your mother taught you how to lead yourself and how to be in control. You were taught to be strong, independent, and self-reliant, which are not necessarily bad characteristics but they're not recipes for healthy relationships. So when you end up getting with a man who knows how to lead you, you will be skeptical of his decisions; you will doubt him and give him resistance every time he tries to lead because your end goal is not to get hurt or end up being in a relationship like the ones you may have witnessed growing up. If you were raised with a father whose leadership style was either autocratic, authoritarian, or laissez-faire, your ability to allow a partner to lead will require conscious awareness of your past experience and a willingness to not repeat your parents' teaching.

A leader who is constantly under scrutiny and who has to fight to make decisions cannot lead effectively, because he or she will waste time arguing and having to acquire approval for every decision he or she wants to make. Whether you are aware of it or not, if you were raised with the mindset to protect yourself and be your own independent woman, unless you are cognizant of your behavior and want better than what your mother had, you will be protecting what you were taught and it won't be easy to be vulnerable and let go in your relationship with your partner. On the other hand, if a man was also raised by his mother, he was taught how to follow a woman and not how to lead one. So by nature, men with that kind of upbringing will either step back and let the woman lead in order to have a relationship with her, or he'll do what he thinks is leading, and expect the woman who was only taught how to lead to follow him. For some men who are attempting to lead by doing the right thing, finding resistance from a leading woman will create doubt and, frustration. Inevitably, he will become fed up and succumb to her ways or leave altogether. And the woman who is able to relinquish her desire to lead may meet with disappointment because the man is not meeting her expectations of being the leader she wants. They both end up not getting much done as a unit because they're both afraid of stepping on each other's toes and creating conflicts or alternatively creating a dysfunctional dynamic.

The takeaway is we have to understand our upbringing. A good leader is as good as his or her follower. Jesus was a leader, but he was crucified because people didn't believe in his message. Conversely, a good follower is only as good as his or her leader. If you weren't taught to be a leader, only you can make the decision to learn what it means to be one and become one. And if you weren't raised to be a follower, you are responsible for learning what it means to be a follower. As the saying goes, leaders are made, not found. Building what we want, something that's different and healthier from any broken and dysfunctional patterns and relationships we may have witnessed growing up, requires awareness and a willingness to be healthier and different. Understanding that our parents gave us the tools that worked or didn't work for them, will actually help us do better. In order to have healthier and more purposeful relationships with the opposite sex, we need to let go of what we were taught as leaders and followers and start our healing process.

Leading is a learned habit, but we all have our roles and parts to play as men and women. In any institution, everyone has their part and role to play. You go to work, you understand how to play your role, you do your job, just as your coworkers do regardless of their titles. For the most part, everyone understands what they're supposed to do. You go to church and if you are part of a group, a team, you play your role and let everybody else play theirs. You play sports, you understand your position and play your role and do what you're supposed to do as required by your position. And when you have to play someone else's position, you still understand it's not your permanent position.

But in relationships, we're somehow taught to reject our roles. We're afraid of not being in control or being controlled and not being equal. We reject the things that make us unique, different, and beautiful. Understanding and playing your role shouldn't make you feel less than the other person. It shouldn't mean that you are the follower or you are the leader. In relationships, we are both leaders and followers. Our children are also leaders and followers and should be raised as such. The pastor leads the church because that's his role, and most of us church folks respect that and honor this. But we somehow reject it in our personal relationships. The president leads the country because that's his role; his subordinates understand that and they understand their roles and they do what they're supposed to do. The farmer leads the farm and makes sure everything is growing properly; that's his role. Every piece of the puzzle makes the puzzle complete. A relationship is no different; but because we think too much and we are too smart, we just complicate it because we are broken. We're hurting too much; we can't be vulnerable. We fight too much for equality and fail to acknowledge and embrace our differences. We have so much fear that we can't let our guard down and let go.

The truth is we are not being taught what our roles are in relationships, so we end up improvising because our parents didn't give us the script. We are learning as we go and a lot of us are rigid in what we were taught; we are not open to change so we end up destroying our own relationships and blame the other person for not being a good leader or follower. We wouldn't be in so much pain if we didn't feel the need to always be on the defensive and choose instead to share our gifts with our partner. Rather than contesting each other's ability to lead and follow, it's best to understand that neither one of you may have been raised with the groundwork to do so. Only by practicing healthier habits will we attain healthier outcomes.

CHAPTER 5

DEFEATED BOYS: BORN GUILTY

WHEN I WAS A TEENAGER, I would look around me, sometimes in despair, thinking of all the young boys my age who had either been in juvenile detention or might end up in the judicial system, not because they were necessarily bad kids, but because of their skin's complexion and being born into the disparity of lacking guidance and financial instability. Being an immigrant from Haiti, I never thought I'd be able to relate to a culture that criminalizes its own citizens by just looking at them. Growing up, if I were ever told that my skin color would be the first impression of who I was, I wouldn't have believed it. In Haiti the majority of the population is of African descent, so we were in the majority. Although lighter-skinned Haitians were seen as superior to those with darker complexions, I wasn't aware of the lingering slavery mindset until I came to America.

I remember having a hard time filling out paperwork because, to me, I wasn't Black, I was Haitian. If anything, I'd probably be dark brown. I would always choose "other" and specify Haitian. I realized that my skin color mattered about a year after being in the United States. I was with my father, on our way to the Department of Motor Vehicles in downtown Boston to take my driving test, and as we got on the bus, I noticed there was an empty seat next to an older Caucasian woman. As I went to sit next to her, she looked at me in disgust, got up, and walked away as if I were worthless and less than human, with no place in the same world as her. I remember looking at my dad who had been here before me and understood the extent of racism. He shook his head and said in Creole, "Pa okipe sa, se moun rasis li ye " ("Don't worry about it, she's just racist").

I couldn't imagine growing up believing that my skin color determined who I was. A few years later, I was telling an African American friend of mine about my experience when I first came to this country. He began expressing his sympathy for me. Although I appreciated his compassion and empathy, I felt more hurt and wounded for him because he never knew anything else other than being Black, a "nigga" in America. Growing up, I was never called a Black Haitian or an African Haitian. I was never looked at in disgust, with repulsion by a group of ignorant folks who felt like I didn't belong in their stolen country because my skin was darker than theirs.

I did not have the disadvantage of not being able to get a good education based on the way I was born—a Black boy. I consider myself fortunate in that respect. Some of the boys I used to hang out with when I came here ended up in jail, because surviving to them meant doing everything imaginable to make it past today. It meant killing and destroying themselves and each other in order to protect themselves and provide for their single parents and siblings living in the projects, caged and surrounded by police officers with no other intent but to lock them up. I guess I was fortunate to have a dad who fought tooth and nail to provide for his family, and a mother who would kill me if I were ever caught doing anything illegal. I also had a moral compass that was clearer than the urge to become what those friends were teaching me.

But a lot of them weren't that lucky. They didn't have that father. They didn't have that mother. They didn't have those grandparents I had growing up in Haiti. They didn't have those memories I had: waking up early, helping my grandfather to feed the animals and cut the weeds so the beans could grow. My friends didn't have teachers who cared about them not missing a school day. They didn't have parents to guide them. Sadly, most of them had the judicial system to keep them at bay when they'd act up and a for-profit place called prison when they expressed frustration about their lives.

Where's Dad?

I used to be angry. Really ANGRY. I swore I would probably kill my biological father if I ever met him. That's how empty I used to feel. I felt unwanted, undeserved, not belonging. I had suicidal thoughts. That used to be me. I remember watching an episode of *The Fresh Prince of Bel-Air* after emigrating to America. The character Will was super excited to go on a trip with his father, but his father, as usual, ended up canceling the trip without even saying goodbye or letting him know. Watching that clip, I could feel Will's hurt and sadness. His disappointment spoke to me, although our situations may have been different; but as an African-descent boy who struggled with those emotions, I felt it. If you haven't seen that episode and you're a boy who's been disappointed and hurt and feels defeated because a father was not around, it's worth a watch.

I didn't like to talk about my problems much, so I kept everything bottled up and blamed myself for everything that happened to me. If my mom was upset and gave me a whupping, it was my fault and I deserved it. If anything went wrong, well, it was because I was around and it was my fault. I carried it all. I took it all in and took it upon myself to fix it and make it okay.

Many boys who grow up without their father, a single mom, or with a mom in an abusive relationship, feel like it's their job to provide for and protect their mothers. Some will even blame themselves and feel the need to do whatever it takes to make it right. As someone whose grandparents raised me until I was about nine years old when I went to live with my mom, those thoughts and feelings were always with me.

I know I was loved by my grandparents, and my grandmother adored me. My maternal grandfather, Esteele, was a farmer. I remember his bald head and sturdy physique. He was an imposing, yet relatable, man, a hard worker, always up before everyone else to take care of his crops and animals. I can still hear my grandmother calling my nickname, "Doudou." She was so sweet. I remember I used to touch her knee because she was ticklish there and she would jump and say, "Oy fout" (I don't even know what that means, but I think it's equivalent to saying "oh shoot" when someone startles you) and we would both laugh hysterically. She was a coffee drinker; I mean, that lady *loved* coffee. She would have it about two to three times a day. I remember she was very slim with short gray natural hair. She was missing a few teeth and her cheeks were a bit droopy, but she was still a beautiful woman with a smile and kindness that welcomed everyone around. Even though we didn't have a lot of material possessions aside from crops and animals, we had love for each other. I remember being content eating fresh mangoes, almonds, coconuts, oranges, and grapefruits. We never had to go hungry, because my grandparents always provided. My grandfather took pride in working hard and taking care of his family. Providing for your family and keeping them safe was what a man does. I had a lot of cousins; some of us would sleep on the same mat made out of dried grass leaves, knotted together by ropes, but we were happy. We had no worries; we were safe, even when necessities like clean water were a couple of miles away. We complained at times, but we knew it was a way of life, a good life and we accepted it. It always puzzles me how people with so much find so little to be grateful for. We'd find joy in the littlest things: the made-up games, the nighttime stories sitting around camp fires, rolling on the grass, and playing soccer with friends. Life was simple, and it was beautiful even without the fancy clothes and belongings.

Moving In with Mom

When I was about nine, I moved in with my mom. She was a good mom and she did her best to give me the life, she felt I needed. But just like anyone who's been through a traumatic experience, she had a lot of pain and hurt that she was holding on to. She had been broken. The shattered dreams, the thought that life would never be the same because she had to become a mother to a child when she herself was a child. It must've hurt like hell, I'm sure. If only I understood then what I understand now. The lonely days I experienced. I took on her guilt and her pain. I felt like I was paying for the sin that my biological father committed. The hurt she was probably feeling then became my hurt because I believed if it hadn't been for me, she wouldn't have been going through the agony of being a teenage mom. I started to question my existence and whether or not there was a purpose for me on this earth.

In most Haitian households, depression was not a thing. Talking about your feelings wasn't really a thing either. Emotionally connecting with your parents wasn't really a thing for most. Displaying love and affection was shown through providing for your family. If you have a roof over your head, food to eat, clothes on your body, then you have nothing to complain about. Don't expect to be heard or understood. In fact, as children, you're not supposed to look at adults in the eyes when they're talking to you; it's considered a sign of disrespect. Don't talk back or speak unless spoken to. But can you blame them? It's what they've been taught. Our ancestors weren't allowed to look at their masters when they were being spoken to. Those traditions, those ways of living and loving, have been passed down from generation to generation. Our parents' parents raised them with the same mindset and attitude, and they end up raising us as such. In other words, we have continued to be slaves by enslaving ourselves, our children, our loved ones, and our minds each and every day.

Everything I was feeling and going through was kept inside. I listened to all those voices telling me who I was and who I was never going to be. But I vividly recall the one thing that was always driving me: the urge to one day make enough money to take care of my mother, to repay her for sacrificing herself to have me. Although the guilt I felt for having been born was psychologically destroying me, it was what kept me pushing through.

Like many athletes and entertainers who were raised by single moms or mothers in toxic relationships or with disappointing fathers around, I wanted a way to fill the voids of being the man that my biological father wasn't and to take care of my mom. For many boys, this is the trap they fall into when their fathers are not in their lives or when their fathers fail to be the man their mothers desire. We guilt ourselves into being men and never learn how to be boys. But, as a boy, it's not your job, it's not your responsibility to replace the father that wasn't around or to make up for the one who didn't know how to be a decent one. You need your chance to be a boy, a kid, someone that should be protected, not the protector. Children need to be loved and nurtured. You need parents who are patient with you, and tell you how proud they are of you. It is tragic when children, like me, feel guilt, anger, defeat, and sometimes worthlessness when you see your mom struggling to make ends meet, alone.

Teaching Your Sons

It was never meant for only one parent to raise a child. But life happens, I get it. Sometimes you have no choice but to do without the other parent. As the African proverb says, "It takes a village to raise a child." In Haiti, I couldn't act a fool, thinking that I was grown and able to do whatever I wanted. Before I even got home, somebody would have already told my grandparents or my mother and, trust me, whatever I'd be doing and thinking was fun would not have been worth it. I respected others because of it. I respected myself because of it. I treated others with kindness because I had the community watching and raising me as well.

In spite of not growing up with my biological father, I was raised by a community that provided some of the things that I needed to fill my emptiness. Nowadays, if you tell a parent about their child misbehaving, they will probably curse you out and tell you to mind your own business. It's disheartening to see parents giving up on their children and letting them do whatever they want, act any way they want, because they love them too much to reprimand or discipline them. As parents, we need to guide our children. You don't have to make every decision for them, but be there to guide them; that's your responsibility to them. You are raising them to be good members of society. You don't have to use physical abuse or shame them, but rather teach them accountability that will keep them safe and humble when they become adults. Teach them responsibility, so when they grow up they will respect themselves and treat others with kindness. Don't shower them with material things you didn't have growing up. That's not you loving them; that's enabling them and crippling them.

I remember meeting a mom who told me how much she loves her two boys and couldn't say no to them. And it was wonderful that she loves them, as she should. But the way she showed them her love was by buying them everything they wanted, by doing everything for them. There's nothing wrong with giving your children something they want if you can afford to, but there's everything wrong with not teaching your children the importance and privilege of getting what they want. What you want are not necessities—they are privileges.

Many parents are so concerned with not being accepted by their children, or wanting to be seen as friends by their children, that they end up raising boys to have a princely mentality. Those boy princes are entitled, they are demanding, they are selfish, and they have narcissistic tendencies. There's nothing wrong with raising masculine boys; they are born with testosterone—but the way they are raised will determine what kind of human beings they will be.

Raise boys who are confident, great leaders, team players, innovators, helpers, and healers. Emotionally and psychologically healthy and masculine boys are kind, loving, and protective; they won't hurt others because they're always in a defensive mode. They will protect those around them because it will bring them great pride and joy to do what is right. They will be receptive to change because they welcome growth. It won't be an easy task. Our culture is teaching our boys that being masculine is toxic. We've created so much confusion that our boys no longer understand what it means to be boys. And we as parents have given up on our sons because we don't understand them—so we've left it up to teachers, friends, and the judicial system to do our job and raise them for us. They need you, their mothers and fathers, even when they act like they're grown men and they know it all. You are still that instruction manual they were born with and that they need to use in order to do what's right. Let's not fail them as parents and guides.

CHAPTER 6

FED-UP MEN

GROWING UP WITHOUT EMOTIONALLY HEALTHY male role models, and seeing mothers taking care of everything and continually finding fault in fathers for not being enough or not doing enough, will produce defeated boys. You start seeing your life as a disappointment, because the man who is supposed to be your hero seems to be failing at nearly everything.

After a while, Dad is no longer around, whether physically or emotionally, because he's fed up with everything. He's fed up with not knowing how to truly show love and affection to either Mom or the kids, because it wasn't something that he was taught or saw while growing up. He left because even though he tried his best to do what he thought was right, it seemed to be never enough. He's fed up with himself and stops trying. And even if he's still around, he seems to be absent emotionally, mentally, spiritually, and psychologically. A lot of African-descent men learn how to be men from their media idols, who may not have been taught what being a man was. They watch those men on television flaunting their shiny jewelry, fancy cars, and mansions, and they aspire to be those men. They take shortcuts to success, grinding and hustling, because they've been taught to "get that money, get that paper, and you'll get all the honeys you want."

Most African-descent men were never taught how to be emotionally decent men, how to create a legacy of kindness, and how to be great providers, loving husbands, and community leaders. A lot of us men are not being taught how to take responsibility for what we do. Many of us bypass the part of our childhood when we needed to learn self-control, how to express our emotions with words, and how to listen and pay attention. For those men who were raised by a parent who was either broken or fed up, learning and mastering these skills would have been nearly impossible.

As a boy who may have been told to man up, that real men don't cry, or to act like a man, you learn to internalize your feelings and keep them bottled up. You get defeated at such an early age; your chances of being an emotionally and psychologically well-rounded man becomes slim to none. You have learned to be fed up with situations that remind you of the defeated experiences you may have gone through as a boy, and consequently you walk away from responsibilities that are yours to take. You use your fists in situations that could have been resolved with simple, logical understandings, if only you were taught as a boy to use your words to express yourself.

Not Having a Male Role Model

Sometimes having a dad or a male role model can be more psychologically, physically, and spiritually detrimental to a boy than it is helpful. A father or a male role model can either teach you how to be a responsible man or an irresponsible one. As children, we learn from what we see and we copy behaviors from those we admire most. As a man, you can aspire to be like your father or you can detest him and everything he stands for, become driven by your pain and hatred for him, and create your own subconscious self-destruction.

Even though I never met my biological father, I was angry and hated everything about him, and that was fundamentally everything I didn't know about him, because I had never met him. I realized for me to be different from my biological father, I needed to let go of that hate. I hated myself more than I hated him because, as I said earlier, I blamed myself for his sins and shortcomings. So I learned to forgive him. I've forgiven him, because forgiving him means forgiving myself. Like it or not, he is part of me, so hating him also means hating that part of me.

Allowing myself to let go of that pain, that self-blame I carried with me throughout my teenage years, was one of the best things I could have ever done for myself. I've forgiven him because letting go of that anger allowed me to have a healthier and deeper love in my heart for my daughter and other meaningful relationships. Even though I had my grandfather growing up, who was a great man, the thought of not having or knowing my biological father affected me deeply. And although I eventually had a great father figure in my life, someone I look up to and respect dearly, certain thoughts I had while growing up never disappeared. So I get it—for most of you men who grew up thinking that it was either your fault or your responsibility to replace your father, I want you to know that in order for you to be the man you aspire to and were meant to be, you have to let go of any residual anger, pain, and resentment. Most African-descent men have no idea how to navigate the world of manhood. We didn't have a blueprint and model to follow so we could understand manhood. Perhaps you grew up in a home that was so dysfunctional and emotionally chaotic and draining, you found refuge in friends, the streets, the basketball team, grandparents, or the community church.

But it's never too late to learn. It's never too late to heal yourself and become a role model for another boy who needs you. It's never too late to create a refuge of your own through healing and purpose. If you want to have that emotional and loving connection with your sons and daughters, you have to find healing and learn how to be the man you were never taught to be. You can be the role model father you wanted growing up by healing yourself and being open to the possibility of becoming someone healthier and better. You can be that exemplary partner by healing yourself and learning how to choose an emotionally healthy and purposeful partner.

Self-Understanding

Due to our racial history and our lack of teaching, not being able to uphold parts of our purpose as men has caused our women to step up and do what we men were created to do: provide for, protect, love, and help raise our sons and daughters. And so, our egos get crushed, our sense of self diminishes, and who we are becomes dubious and purposeless. This lack of competence and self-sufficiency has caused some men to become abusive, controlling, insecure, and stuck in a psychological spin cycle. Without taking any necessary steps towards self-healing and self-discovery, we end up in dysfunctional or toxic romantic relationships and blame one another for our lack of self-understanding and self-fulfillment. We end up with a woman whom society has taught to value men for their possessions, as well as for their potential to give her what she wants, say the right things, and satisfy her emotionally. Again, when this happens, you start feeling unappreciated, undervalued, and unloved in spite of your efforts. Your journey towards your purpose starts vanishing because you no longer recognize who you are and all your gifts, which keeps you from living your purpose.

Being in a romantic relationship with someone can either give birth to your dreams or kill them the moment you relinquish your heart and soul to that person. Imagine having the wrong friends, who encourage you to do irresponsible and unconstructive things instead of encouraging you to succeed and be better. Being in a relationship can have that much power over your life, your goals, your present, and your future, especially when you go into it already hurting and broken. You're giving somebody permission to hurt you and to carry you or to drop you if they choose to. You're giving somebody your home, your fortress with everything inside of it, your heart, your soul, your mind, your spirit, your life, which they can choose to either maintain and improve or destroy. As men, most of us are not equipped to handle and understand our own emotions, let alone a woman's emotions, just like most women are not equipped to understand themselves as well as men. In a way, we're not feeling for ourselves; we're being told when, why, how, and what to feel. Boys are given "manly" toys to play with and told not to show weaknesses. They are told to man up, conquer the world, sow wild oats, build and break stuff, and not show their feelings. On the other hand, girls are taught to be feminine, play with dolls, watch shows that are about princesses and princes. We are never taught how to accept and understand each other's world.

In general, every man wants to satisfy and please his woman. Every man wants to feel like he's doing the right things to bring her joy. But because of the disparity between men and women, we will always find it extremely difficult to find, create, and maintain healthy relationships. The problem lies in the teaching and upbringing of men and women. Boys are not taught how men to treat women properly and girls are not taught how to treat men appropriately. We can't change a broken cycle if we're not willing to let go of our toxic ways and destructive behaviors. If women expect men to be clueless when they meet them, the more clueless the men will be. The more you tell someone they can't do something, the least likely they will believe they should even try. The more you expect someone to fail at something, all you will focus on is the failure. And sadly, a lot of men believe and accept that they are just simply clueless, partially because they would rather not have to deal with a woman's emotions.

Being with You

There are several reasons why most African-descent men feel out of place in their relationships with the African-descent woman. If we are to progress and generate healing and healthy changes, we as a people need to collectively look at ourselves, not only from our own biased and wounded standpoints but from those who love us and whom we love. For one, we have been pitted against each other for way too long, and we won't go back to one another without understanding the detrimental and painful ways we love, treat, and interact with one another.

Another reason is that the African-descent man doesn't know how to satisfy the African-descent woman. With so many societal expectations and social norms, love, respect, sacrifice, commitment, and understanding are no longer pillars of a relationship. In addition to the fact that we are dealing with the lack of parental examples of how to love and have healthy relationships, we are also compromised by the blurred and shallow teachings of modern civilization. Every commercialized holiday, every idealistic movie depicting the definition of love and romance, creates more confusion and unrealistic expectations that most men can't achieve. We feel inadequate, incompetent, frustrated, fed up, and failing at the one thing that was meant to be natural. We are expected to be like the romantic men portrayed in the movies, on TV, the Internet, or in magazines. Most of us are failing at love and relationships because our understanding of them has been commercialized and monetized. We no longer think, see, and process our lives with purpose. In spite of our efforts to satisfy you, sacrifice for you, and do what we think is right, it just seems to never be enough.

Another problem is that the African-descent man fears the African-descent woman. As an African-descent man, I love African-descent women like I love my mother—with respect, protection, provision, caring, and all of my pain. Loving you feels effortless, but being with you doesn't always feel easy and peaceful. Our history is partly to blame; you don't always feel protected by us because we couldn't protect you. We don't always provide what you desire from us because for so long we couldn't, and some still can't. Our fears come from our own insecurities about being men and being everything society expects us to be. The way you love us with your strength and wounds, we don't always know how to navigate through them. And it shouldn't be our job to fix it, just like it's not your job to raise any half-raised men. As I mentioned before, there's a saying that goes "hurt people hurt people"—so the more you're hurting, the more you consciously and subconsciously hurt those closest to you.

When your pain turns into anger and aggression, for those men who were raised by a hurting mother or in a household that was dysfunctional, your aggression and irritation become triggers. Ultimately, you'll feel unheard, unloved, unappreciated, and disrespected, and we both end up hurting because we don't know how to handle each other's pain. We both need healing if we're ever going to feel connected and safe with each other. Even though we've espoused a "happy wife, happy life" dysfunctional mentality—when we should be promoting a "happy spouse, happy house" mindset—it is not your job to make us happy, whole, complete, or to heal us, just like it is not ours to do those things for you. None of us is equipped to heal pain we don't understand. We can help each other heal, grow, and reach our purpose; but if we believe that we are the source of each other's pain, helping each other heal and grow together won't be achievable.

Your View of Us

In spite of how we may feel about each other, the way we love one another, our disconnect, and our broken bonds, your opinion of us matters. We care deeply about how you feel about us and we always have you in the back of our minds in nearly everything we do. The thought of you motivates us, empowers us, pushes us to do more, and encourages us. But sometimes those thoughts can break us down, strip us away of our confidence, make us insecure, and even create havoc. As men, whom society is so eager to break down because our masculinity and skin complexion are deemed toxic and threatening, we need you just like you need us.

I get that it's not easy to cheer us on when you are hurting, and when we are causing you more pain because of what we're not being taught as men by our fathers. But speaking from a man's point of view, being encouraged by you inspires us to be more and do more, to love you better and feel safer with you. Growing up, some of us had a mother—our biggest fan—to cheer us on. Whether it was our moms, our dads, or our grandparents, it's so important to have someone to say, "You can do it, I believe in you, keep going." If you played sports, then it was your coach and your teammates. And if you exercise at a gym, you have other members or maybe trainers who say, "One more rep, you got this, come on, keep pushing, that was good, you killed it." That positive energy, those affirmations, push you to go further and motivate you to do more: to get that last rep in, run those extra yards, conquer the world.

Likewise, as a friend, a partner, a spouse, we need you in order for us to be better for you, to feel more connected to you, to be able to protect you more. But if we feel like we are disappointments to you—the one person who is supposed to be our ultimate cheerleader, our ultimate fan, our support system—if you are booing us for not doing enough, for not meeting your expectations, we won't have much to give you. No one who feels depleted, defeated, and hopeless will feel motivated to give his or her best, and that includes you. Whether you're a man or a woman, we need each other's support. We need to be each other's cheerleader, instead of pointing out each other's shortcomings and inadequacies.

The Simplicity of Most Men

Men don't need much. They don't ask for much. They don't require much to feel satisfied. They just want a stable life and peace of mind. But I believe there are two different kinds of men: the traditional man and the modern man. The traditional man wants to find a good job, create opportunities, find an emotionally healthy woman, and have a family. He wants to provide, protect, eat, sleep, have sex, be understood, and be emotionally supported. His home is his castle where he is the king. But the modern man wants to have it all—the looks, the shines, the bells and whistles. He is the conqueror. He wants to have it and he wants it to be all about him. The modern man has what I call the Prince Syndrome.

Growing up, these types of men didn't have to assume any responsibilities. They weren't held accountable for their actions; they were Mama's Prince Charming. They got whatever they wanted, whenever they wanted it. They had expensive things and thought those things were easily afforded. While most men take pride in protecting and providing, these princes want to be catered to; they like to receive, and eventually they find a woman who is a replacement for whomever raised them to be that way. The traditional man, on the other hand, was taught to take care of those around him: to be caring, protective, kind, and giving. But unfortunately, whatever the type of man he is, he's not taught to understand a woman's emotions. A man can't outtalk a woman during a disagreement, especially if logic no longer applies. So when a man stops talking, it's not because he thinks the woman is right; most of the time he just doesn't want a confrontation that he knows won't lead to a positive outcome.

And truth is, the moment a man starts being silent, it is the beginning of the end of the relationship. He no longer feels safe expressing himself. He no longer feels heard, respected, and valued. He no longer sees you, the woman, whom he's sharing his gifts with, as someone he can go to for comfort or peace. You're no longer his haven. And when that happens, even when he's around physically; emotionally, spiritually, and psychologically, he's no longer there.

Understanding that your man also shares the leadership role in the family benefits everyone. When a strong, independent woman says, "I have to make sure he's a leader before I let him lead me and my family," he also must feel like he has a follower in order to lead. Oftentimes we make our relationship unnecessarily unhealthy because we were taught that relationships are not easy. If I'm walking alone, I'm not leading anyone, even though I may be a great leader; but if two leaders are fighting to lead, then we both become followers, and every plan and mission will fail and end up on separate paths.

No man who is about creating a life of purpose will spend his time and energy fighting the woman he chose to share his gifts with in order to gain leadership of his safe haven. It is wasted time and energy, and it isn't worth it. If you undermine his decisions, you can't expect him to keep making decisions. If you dismiss his way of leading, you can't expect him to take the lead. If you minimize his plans, you can't expect him to keep trying. Men don't function that way. Even during sex, he will be open to learning how to please you better if he feels like he's doing something right. When you appreciate what he does, you will get more out of him. Part of the reason a lot of women can't get their man to do what they want him to do is because they lack sensuality. They think being feminine and easygoing and caring makes them weak. It doesn't. It makes you smart. It makes you satisfied. I know you're probably thinking it's all about you doing for the man, but it's not.

A man who wants you will do anything he has to do to get with you—but you can't expect him to keep working to get you if you don't do anything to keep him. His tank needs gas, too. He needs to feel loved and appreciated, too. Not just reminders of what he's not doing right and how unromantic he is, or how he doesn't take the trash out or put down the toilet seat every time he uses it. Society expects a lot of him and sometimes he gets tired, especially when he doesn't feel like he's getting it right. Don't be society to him; don't beat him up too.

Even when society is trying to destroy his masculinity, a masculine man will always protect and preserve a feminine woman. An insecure man will fight you and fight with you, but a masculine man wants you to be protected and provided for, in whatever capacity he can. But no man will fight for you if all you do is fight him. No man will advocate for you when all you do is belittle and emasculate him. And no man will protect you when he himself doesn't feel safe with you. Raise your sons to be masculine men. Breathe life and masculinity into your man. There's nothing worse than having a silent man in your household. You may not realize that your family is falling apart when your man becomes silent, but trust me, it is. So as his refuge, as his peace, as his feminine side, let him see you for the woman that you are meant to be, not what society is teaching you to be; not the fighter you were taught to be; not the strong woman you have become in order to survive your childhood traumas; not the independent woman you learned to become in order to survive your past experiences; not the always-giving-a-piece-of-your-mind woman you had to be in order to protect yourself. Be the woman you were meant to be. The peaceful woman, the kind woman, the purposeful woman, the loving woman, the nurturing woman, the caring woman, the content woman, the woman that brings you and your environment peace and love.

Having a healthy relationship is only as easy or as hard as you both make it. It takes as much work as you want it to take. Date night shouldn't feel like work. Taking vacations shouldn't feel like work. Appreciating your mate shouldn't take work. When you do the right thing, you don't have to work hard to do it. You have to learn the right things in order to do the right things. We should heal ourselves, become healthier so we can pass down to our children and future generations healthier habits and generational mental stability so they won't have to go through as much depression, anxiety, and chaos as we did.

CHAPTER 7

LOVE YOUR PARENTS, LOVE YOUR CHILDREN

MOST OF US DON'T UNDERSTAND how to parent our children healthily and purposefully. There's a Haitian proverb that says, "Pitit se riches malerez" (Children are the wealth of the poor). When I was growing up, I didn't really understand the true meaning of that proverb. My interpretation, like most Haitians and African-descent families, was that people have children so they can help their parents live a better life, take care of them, and financially provide for them in ways their parents couldn't provide for themselves.

Many African-descent parents end up holding their children captive and feeling guilty about the things their parents had done for them during their childhood. Things like feeding, clothing them, putting them through school, and giving them what they need. For a lot of African-descent parents, children should be indebted to them for being responsible parents. But as I got older and became a dad, I realized my understanding of that proverb was entirely wrong. The wealth one gets from children is not financial. The joy that my daughter adds onto my life is beyond anything that money could buy me. The joy of spending time with her and loving her and watching her develop day after day into the smart, sweet, kind, generous little girl is invaluable.

If all we have to give our children is our hurt and misery, our anger, frustrations, and disappointments, we are robbing them of their emotional wealth. Giving them our love is showering them with our riches. Some families who don't have the means to pass down to them, expect their children to get it and pass it up to them, which is truly unfair. Your children shouldn't have to feel the need to pay you back for sharing your gifts with them, for allowing them to read the manual they came with. Those are the instructions I talked about earlier, which you hold as the people who have been blessed with the opportunity to guide their journey and lead them in ways that are going to help them serve their purpose. Our children owe us nothing but appreciation and respect for our sacrifices as parents. They owe us love and kindness—but we first need to show them, by the way we love and treat them and how we love and treat ourselves and those around us. We must live our lives in a way that tells them, without having to say anything, that we are healthy living examples of how they can live their purpose.

I've spoken to children who are not proud of their parents' unhealthy and destructive behaviors, and it's damaging to them, spiritually and mentally. Let's not lose our children because we have lost ourselves. By changing our unhealthy patterns and by living healthier and more purposeful lives, we can guide them better and help them create healthier connections and more meaningful relationships. Let's not allow our own self-interest to guide our children into serving our own purpose instead of raising and guiding them to discover their own.

Smart Generations

It's no secret that we have lost a great deal of what used to be human connection and emotional maturity. As beneficial as technological advancement has been, human connection and interaction has taken a setback. Some of us think we're so smart that we treat our parents as if they never experienced a life of their own. My daughter is four years old and the smartest kid I know (I'm not just saying that, she really is); but even at four, her concept of knowing everything can sometimes be bewildering. Her mother and I would never want to take that confidence away from her, but part of our responsibilities is to teach her humility, and a desire to keep her a curious learner without breaking down her spirit or taking away her enthusiasm for learning. As parents, we are responsible for giving our children healthy emotional and psychological wealth if we want them to share that wealth with us and others. Not financial guilt, not emotional and psychological debts, but the things that money can never buy—psychological stability. Our children will always be more technologically advanced than we are, but if we allow ourselves to let technology take away what we were meant to be for them and to them, we are doing them a disfavor. As children, we may think everything can be found with a quick click of the mouse and it can replace the wisdom of our parents; but this belief will only lead us to emotional emptiness and chaos. We need to stop creating barriers that prevent us from having that emotional and psychological connection we so crave for with each other.

Children Become Their Parents

I know this won't resonate well with some folks because the idea of them being anything like their mother or father will appall them, but stay with me. You've probably heard the saying "a father is his daughter's first love, and a mother is her son's first love." If this is true, how are we as parents teaching our sons and daughters what loving themselves and others truly means? What kind of outline are we illustrating to guide them in their own personal relationship with the world, with their friends, and with a potential mate? Now, before we move forward, let's understand what love means. I'm not talking about a one-dimensional kind of love. Loving your children and loving your parents falls into the category of the most meaningful and substantial kind of love. And although the simple definition of love is the act of sacrificing for oneself or for others, understanding and learning healthy ways to express and accept love will simplify and improve your relationships.

Let's start with one of my favorite types of love.

Philautia

This kind of love is self-love and it can be healthy or unhealthy, depending on how loving yourself helps you view and deal with yourself and the world around you. Most of us don't realize how important it is to love yourself. I believe self-love is the most important kind of love. The way you love, treat, and see yourself will be a reflection of how you seek to be loved and how you love others. It doesn't mean you won't crave a different or a healthier kind of love if you don't know how to love yourself in a healthy way—but it's extremely difficult for others to give you the love you're craving until you learn how to truly love yourself like you crave to be loved. Others will treat and love you the way you love and treat yourself. When you love yourself and live a peaceful, purposeful, fulfilled life, you know what is healthy and good for you and what isn't; you know who enhances your peace and how to avoid those who don't; you know whom to allow into your life and whom not to. When you love yourself, you understand kindness is not weakness. You won't need to hurt others to feel better about yourself. However, an unhealthy concept of love for oneself can also lead to selfishness, narcissism, and an utter lack of empathy for others. The key is to aim for psychological and emotional health while seeing, treating, and carrying yourself in loving ways that benefit not just you, but those around you.

Agape

If you understand the concept of godly love, this should be a no brainer. If you love God unconditionally and God loves you unconditionally, then loving your children, loving your parents and loving others should be your priority, even with their imperfections and shortcomings. (Reminder: loving others doesn't mean you are obligated to share your gifts with them, nor does it mean you should allow them to take away your peace of mind or deter you from living in your purpose.) The way you love your children is the way they're going to learn to love others and themselves. The idea of loving others unconditionally makes perfect sense when it is understood. If you love someone unconditionally, you learn to accept them. You show them kindness even when they don't necessarily deserve it. You extend grace even when it's not easy. You are truthful with them even when it doesn't serve you. And you make sacrifices for them directly or indirectly. That said, loving others unconditionally must come with boundaries in order to protect and preserve loving yourself unconditionally.

Loving your children and your parents unconditionally doesn't mean you can't hold them accountable when they fall short and make mistakes or act in ways that hurt you. It doesn't mean we love them because they're perfect and will never do wrong or cause us hurt. They're still human, they are still from the same tree that birthed us, sins and all. But in order for our children to learn what that kind of love is, we need to show them how to properly love. There is no love in physical and verbal abuse. There is no love in anger, control, jealousy, or any unhealthy emotional behavior. The foundation you build for them and for yourself is how you will teach your children to express and receive love.

Eros

This is the romantic/sexual, passionate kind of love. As a self-proclaimed pragmatist, the idea of romance, and the destructive habits it creates in our society, actually makes me cringe. Don't get me wrong, I believe in doing thoughtful acts to show your mate how much you appreciate their sacrifices and the privilege of sharing each other's gifts. But the concept of romance has been socially constructed by Western civilization, selfishly commercialized, materialized, and emotionalized in ways that are repulsive to me.

If you are a true believer of romance, it's about fairy tales; and if these fairy tales truly work for you and your loved ones, I won't take that away from you. But the point here is to understand that our idea of romantic love comes from what we have learned as children—watching movies and shows depicting princesses and princes saving each other and doing these fairy tale acts that speak to our sentimental and emotional fantasies. So, if you are a parent, you can teach and educate your children about the kind of love that is different from what we see in fairy tale flicks and scripted stories. That will save them from accumulating a load of emotional and psychological disappointments and emptiness in their adult life when they fail to receive the kind of romantic love that had been advertised and sold to them. We can teach them how to truly appreciate those who are willing to make genuine sacrifices for them and share their gifts of life with them.

Mothers, if you are in a relationship, it's up to you to show your sons how a woman should appreciate and love a man by the way you appreciate and passionately love the man in your life, rather than how a woman is supposed to be romantically loved by a man. Your sons need to witness how an emotionally and psychologically healthy and stable woman treats a man. Also, as mothers it's your job to teach your daughters how to affectionately treat and love a potential mate and how to be an emotionally healthy and well-rounded woman in a passionate relationship. Fathers, it's your job to teach your daughters how they should be treated by a potential mate by the way you passionately love, treat, protect, and provide for the women in your life, including your partner and mother. The way you love them is what they'll crave when they start dating. It is also your duty to teach your sons how a man should act by the way you act. Sons will learn how a man should treat and appreciate a mate by the way you treat, appreciate, and care for the women in your life.

Philia

This is affectionate love and fond friendship. I get this kind of love from my daughter; it's cute, it's sincere, and it's heartwarming. Have you ever been in a relationship with someone who is stone cold? That was me. In theory, I knew what to say. As a poet, I could write it. It was easier to express myself that way. In the Haitian culture, showing affection and vulnerability, especially by men, was just not a thing for the most part. Even though I would write love poems and love songs for my partners, expressing how much I cared and cherished them and how much they meant to me, being vulnerable and affectionate was not something I was taught or witnessed growing up. Conversely, women weren't taught how to receive affection because they never had it from Dad, or never learned how to show it because Mom didn't show vulnerability. But it's something that we still crave, especially when we see it in movies, blogs, and magazines, or when other people are displaying it.

As parents, we have a responsibility to raise emotionally healthy and balanced children. Be affectionate to your partner and to your loved ones; it's not weird to show kindness, love and all that mushy mushy stuff. It won't always be easy, especially if you're in place of hurt and disappointment, but it is necessary if you want that kind of relationship with your children, your parents, your partner, and others around you. I'm still learning. I remember I had a close male friend, who was like my big brother. He was affectionate and caring to me, which made me uncomfortable. As a man, I was always taught to be tough, and not to show emotions and affection, especially to other guys. And being affectionate to a woman outside of sex was also not something that was taught or displayed by parents. Our friendship ended, partly because of our differences about showing emotions and being affectionate as men. I'm here to tell you, as a man and a father, whether or not you believe in showing love through affection or emotional vulnerability, creating that emotionally healthy bond with your sons and daughters will help them be secure in themselves and their ability to love and be loved.

Storge

This is natural, familiar love. It's the love that parents and children should have for one another. It's natural, so you shouldn't have to force it; you shouldn't have to feel like you have to work for it; it should be something that feels right when you're emotionally healthy. It's the kind of familiar love that creates unbreakable bonds and strong support systems. For some of us, that storgic love has been damaged and even broken due to our generational, parental, and cultural hurt and teachings. Lack of trust, inherited brokenness, and chaos have destroyed that love, but as parents and children, it is our responsibility to work together, find healing, and rebuild this kind of love that will collectively help us grow and become emotionally healthier.

Parents, we are responsible for how our children's lives will be emotionally structured in their adulthoods. Parenting your children in ways that are healthy and emotionally stable is such a huge task that we should not take it lightly. As I mentioned before, if we have been given the amazing gift of bringing into this world a child and raising another human being, shaping them to be either well rounded or emotionally, spiritually, and psychologically wounded, we must heal ourselves before embarking on that journey. Building a strong kind of love between parents and children is crucial when it comes to raising emotionally stable, self-sufficient children.

Pragma

This is practical/enduring love. You know the sayings "love conquers all" and "love makes the world go 'round." In our culture, we are taught that love is work; if you want something, you have to work for it. But I think love should be something that no one should have to work for. Love was given to us when we were created, just like breath was given to us. If you have to work to breathe, then something is wrong. I'm not saying that you shouldn't have to make sacrifices for love, because if you understand what love is, then you'll understand that love is sacrificing something for someone; it is prioritizing. The Bible illustrates that well: "For God so loved the world, that he gave his only begotten Son, that whosoever believeth in him should not perish, but have everlasting life" (John 3:16). That was a sacrifice of love. And if you're not a biblical person, think about how sometimes you have to sacrifice your whole world in order to create a completely different world with someone else; that's not work, that's sacrificing. You sacrifice the world for your children; that's love. When you have a love that is healthy enough to endure the sacrifices that need to be made and required to survive, you don't take it for granted.

It's when parents choose to pay for their children's tuition instead of buying a new car; that's sacrifice. It's when parents go hungry so their children don't have to; that's sacrifice. It has nothing to do with work; it's sacrificing and doing what is needed in order to preserve love. It's enduring life's unexpected occurrences because that's what love does. Enduring love is not creating hardships and chaos and expecting someone to work for your love. Enduring love is not having to hate yourself in order to endure and work for someone else's love. Enduring love is not putting up with someone else's abusive and destructive ways because you think that's what love requires.

And lastly, enduring love is not detrimental to your health, mind, body and soul. Enduring love gives you courage to keep going by refueling your tank with kindness, empathy, support, understanding, and appreciation. Enduring love strengthens your resilience to get up and try again when you get knocked down. Enduring love sees the sacrifices that are being made and understands that it's not work that sustains the love, but rather the willingness to keep surrendering to the power of creating a healthy and lasting bond. It's about climbing mountains and crossing oceans together for the sake of living purposeful lives. It's about helping and healing oneself and others; building and creating meaningful, undying memories together.

Ludus

This is playful love. If you find yourself working for love, you are not living in love; you are surviving love and may be in a very unhealthy and damaging situationship. Remember when you first fell in love and everything was easy, with no high expectations? You appreciated the littlest of things; you smiled and laughed together. You found nearly everything your lover did or said endearing. Hours on the phone felt like minutes. That playful love encouraged you even when you'd be competing at playing a silly game. Don't lose that. Many of us, at some point, start putting chains on each other because we start owning one another. We start letting all of our pain, insecurities, past mistakes, selfishness, and unrealistic expectations dictate how we treat one another. Most, if not all, of the playfulness, the unwavering respect, and the grace we used to extend to them no longer exists. When we love an emotionally broken person, at some point that initial playful stage ends, and the person starts using all of his or her brokenness as ropes to tie us down. Suddenly love becomes work, I mean serious business—and before you know it, being with that person becomes emotionally draining and a burden. As parents, that's the kind of love we unconsciously end up teaching our children when we aren't emotionally and spiritually healthy. Be playful, create laughter, find joy in the smallest of things, and appreciate one another, and the gifts they'll receive from you will be unparalleled.

Mania

This is obsessive love. To be obsessed with anything or anyone can be extremely unhealthy and flat-out dangerous, but there's a silver lining to this kind of love. Even if you love someone or something unconditionally, and you find them irresistible, too much of even a good thing is good for nothing. Finding balance in the ways that we love ourselves and others is the end goal. But let's think back when we were teenagers, or even kids, before we accumulated disappointments and hurt. Our first love was pure; it was nothing but hearty emotions and unpolluted love. Being around them, thinking about them, speaking of them, would bring fire to our eyes and soul. Then our selfish ways kick in; our bad habits take over, and, before we know it, we are reminded of our brokenness and hurt all over again. Being obsessed is not necessarily the issue; being obsessed without balance, and with the wrong person or detrimental patterns, is the issue. Letting our obsessions become possessive is the issue. We become obsessed with who and what makes us feel good and valuable; so if you are an emotionally healthy individual and understand that you are responsible for your own healthy mind, body, and spirit, having a balanced obsession with your loved ones can be a great thing. It can be shown through appreciation, quality time spent, and being eager to create healthy, meaningful memories. Don't be afraid to obsessively love and cherish the ones you love, as they're not here forever.

Sacrificial Love

I believe this is the most sensible and meaningful kind of love. Unfortunately, it is the one that most of us are lacking and the one we're not being taught. When God sacrificed his only begotten son, it wasn't a sacrifice we deserved, but it was his way of proving his love for us. We were given this gift called life. We didn't have to work for it, we didn't need to ask for it; it's not because we deserved it, but it was given to us with a simple purpose: the intent to use it to help and heal others, to live it by creating healthy memories, and to use it as a sacrificial symbol of love. We can never be like the Son of God and sacrifice that gift to save others, but our actions and commitment to ourselves and others can represent that sacrifice. Most of us have been taught to undervalue this kind of love because it's not always romantic; it doesn't always focus on our wants; it doesn't always know the right things to say according to our expectations, and therefore it's not always rewarded.

Think of the sacrifices a woman has to make to have a child, knowing her body may never be the same again. She gives up her freedom for the responsibility of breastfeeding and nurturing her child. A man has to make sacrifices to take on the responsibility of having a family, knowing that he is partly responsible for keeping them safe. Providing for them means giving up his freedom, his desires for instant gratification. That's sacrificial love. The lack of sacrificial love, and our lack of appreciation for it, is often the reason our relationships fail. As Christians and believers, we glorify, worship, and love Jesus Christ for sacrificing his life for our sins; but we fail to appreciate our spouses, friends, and loved ones for sacrificing their time, their freedom, their bodies, and their gifts to make our lives easier. We take for granted their sacrifices because we feel entitled to their gifts.

Because of our emptiness and deeply rooted pain, and society's detrimental and unrealistic definition of love, we find ourselves spinning in circles, craving objectified and fantasized connections that none of us can attain. What if we could appreciate others the way we appreciate God for his sacrificial love? What would happen if we could learn to see the sacrifices that others make, like we recognize the sacrifice Jesus made on that cross? And what if we could see more than just our own sacrifices? How grateful would we have been? How kind and loving would we be if we could see and embrace that sacrificial love in those closest to us, instead of tumbling into our destructive desire for materialistic, fanciful, unattainable fulfillment? I guarantee you we'd love with less expectation and entitlement. We'd appreciate more and demand less. We'd do our ultimate best to achieve more, because life would be purposeful and relationships would be fulfilling. We'd share more, because we'd have less fear of being taken advantage of and being used for others' own gratifications. We'd be less afraid to love and share our gifts with someone.

Whom Do You Put First?

Whom do you put first: your children or your spouse? The answer is probably both. If both you and your spouse understand the concept of loving your children, you will understand that the act of loving each other is actually loving your children, and vice versa. You cannot truly love and put each other first without loving and putting your children first. Loving your children and putting them first becomes a common denominator because you both want what's best for them. Children are happiest and emotionally healthier when they witness their parents being loving, affectionate, respectful, and kind towards one another. A son is more inclined to treat his mother with love and respect when he sees his father treating and loving his mom with kindness, care, and tenderness. And sons also learn what kind of men they should aspire to be when they grow up by watching how their fathers behave towards women—just like a daughter learns to appreciate, respect, and love her father when she sees her mom treating her father with that same kindness and veneration. She is basing her views of men and relationships based on her parents' relationship.

The love and admiration you have for your spouse is, and should be, different from the one you have with your children. Both fulfill a different space in your life. Some of us love our children so much so that we treat them like they are our best friends and there is no space left for a spouse and mate. Because we've grown up so empty and broken, we find comfort in our children because we feel safer with them. But by doing so, we are subconsciously placing a heavy burden on them; they were never meant to play this role in our lives. They are forced to grow up feeling responsible for helping us heal, or we've learned to weaponize them for our own self-gain. When you learn to love your children the healthy way, without imposing your own self-interests on them, you will learn whom you have to put first. When you and your spouse have a connection above and beyond the children, you will never have to wonder whether or not you should put each other *before* the children. Loving each other shouldn't take away from the love you have for your kids; in fact, it should help strengthen the bond you share as a unit. And your children will love you more because they'll love you without the guilt of having to choose one parent over the other. My advice is to heal yourself enough so you don't have to use your children to fill the emptiness you are feeling or to escape from your partner.

Conditional Love

It always kills me when I hear people say they love their parents because of all the things they've done for them; or even worse, when they show little to no appreciation for their parents because they failed to provide for them in a way they felt entitled to. As a parent, my goal is to raise an emotionally, physically, and spiritually well-rounded human being, by first being my healthiest self and by living a purposeful life. My purpose is to give my daughter every necessary tool she needs to follow a path that leads her to her purpose. And as a son, I understand that my grandparents and my mother did their best to raise me. My mother may not have taught me the most emotionally healthy habits, but she made sacrifices the moment she decided to alter up her life by sharing it with me; that's love. Our parents make sacrifices for us, whether those sacrifices are healthy or not. We should be appreciative because our turn will come to do for them what they did for us; it's a cycle. As the Haitian proverb says, "Bourik fe pitit se pou do li ka repose" (A donkey has offspring so its back may rest). Caring for your parents in their old age is part of your purpose. It may not be financial support. It may not even be physically taking care of them; but if you understand and respect the cycle of life, we are created to take care of each other. You should love your parents because they are your parents, not because of what they did or didn't do, could have or couldn't have done, for you.

Their purpose was to care for you, guide you, and allow you to read the instructions you came with. You don't know what kind of emotional pain they may have been going through or went through as children. When you learn to love and forgive your parents, you carry no burdens for their shortcomings. I wish we would all heal ourselves emotionally, spiritually, and physically before bringing a child into this world. But if that was not the case for your parents, hopefully it will be for you. Love them despite their imperfections and failures; they need it more than you know. But more so, for your peace of mind, just remember to set boundaries. It doesn't mean you owe them anything but your sacrificial love—whatever that love looks like, as long as it doesn't hinder your ability to love yourself and prioritize your peace of mind. Broken people do broken things. They attract brokenness and end up more broken. By having a loving or even a functional relationship with your parents, you are healing yourself and giving yourself room to grow into the person you were meant to be.

CHAPTER 8

GENERATIONAL PAIN: MY FATHER'S SON

I WAS LISTENING TO AN interview with a young Black comedian on a popular radio station in New York City one day. He grew up without his father in his life. He was talking about how he hated that brother ("nigga"), how f*ed up that brother was, and how much he takes care of his mother, his queen. Now, while I empathize with him and truly feel his pain, resentment, and anger for having to take on a role that was never his to take on and for having to miss out on experiencing his father's love, guidance, and instruction manual, he is that brother who will likely become a different version of his father. As I said about my own biological father, when you hate the person who gave you at least 50 percent of your DNA, you also hate part of yourself. I was emotionally and psychologically allowing that detestation I carried inside of me for so many years to subconsciously dictate how I lived my life and how I viewed the world around me. When you allow such hate to manifest inside of you, it drives you to act out.

I was so determined never to be like my biological father that I focused most of my energy on avoiding anything that was going to put me in a position to become him. I avoided committed relationships for a long time because I feared the responsibility that came with it. Hate for a parent can blindfold you, take away your vision, and cloud your clarity. I wanted to hurt someone I had never met. I wanted to avenge my mother for being done wrong, when I didn't know the full story. I eventually realized I was angry for me, for my hurt, my disappointments. I was angry for not having a life with the man who was supposed to teach me what it means to be a man. I was angry for feeling rejected and abandoned by the person who holds the instructions I came with, who gave me that part of genetic material I was born with, those footsteps I was supposed to follow as my guide and bridged my purpose. I decided to forgive him and to work on my healing process by letting go of every perception I had of him; everything I thought I knew; every story I made up; every desire to avenge and cause hurt. I chose healing.

If you never heal from what or who hurt you, you will continue to create hurt for yourself and to those who love you and are trying to love you. It doesn't mean you will forget what they did or allow them to hurt you again; but forgiveness allows you to control whether or not you allow someone's action to continue to hurt you. Forgiveness gives you the power to release and let go of someone or people who did you wrong; it allows you to extend grace instead of hate. It allows you to also give yourself grace when you hurt others and learn from your own actions. Until then, you will teach your children from a place of hurt, you will love others from a place of hurt, because your source of love and teaching will come from fear of not repeating someone else's mistakes. It is time to release and heal.

Emotional Outlet

As comforting as it may be to have children you can confide in or share your burdens with, being mindful of their mental health as parents should be your core priority, especially when it comes to complaining about or condemning their other parent. Your views of their other parent will help dictate how they shape their lives in regard to whom they want or don't want as future relational partners based on your perceptions. The dynamic of growing up in a two-parent household is beneficial in the sense that children get to read both aspects of their manuals, whether negative or positive. A father might express his love as a provider and protector with fear and intimidation instead of with grace, understanding, and emotional connection. That fear creates boundaries and rules to live by, guidelines to follow as long as you are under that roof.

However, that authoritarian tough love also creates anger, hurt, resentment, disconnect, and emotional turmoil. Parents may find themselves on opposite sides of the spectrum when one parent is all about rules and the other parent is about grace and forgiveness. When parents don't know how to work together for the greater good of the children and the family, the children will gravitate towards the parent they feel safer with, especially if they see that parent as a victim. By doing so, those children will start helping that parent carry his or her hurt, anger, frustration, and disappointment.

The moment you start telling a child how the other parent hurt you, you start embedding them into your pain. They will feel the need to become your protector while developing negative views of their other parent. And the role model they should have had to look up to has then become someone whom they have to rescue. Children internalize hurt more than we care to acknowledge and those hurts become the source of their emotional derailment. Every child, regardless of how old he or she may be, wants to know that his or her parents have a healthy relationship.

After I left Boston and moved to New York City, I got a phone call from one of my younger brothers. He was frantically crying. Mind you, he was in his late teens, and a tough football-playing kid. After getting him to calm down a bit, he told me our parents had gotten into an altercation, which nearly got physical. My first instinct was to catch a bus for Boston right away. I was concerned, hurt, and confused because I had never seen my parents argue with each other in a destructive way, at least not in front of us. Although it only takes one time to create a lasting psychological scar, constantly living in it as a child can make you feel immune, and, if you have not yet healed, it can potentially become what your children end up living through. As parents, we have to understand that our children internalize our pain and dysfunctional relationships and make them their own, even when they don't express it. It doesn't matter how old you are; unless you heal from your childhood brokenness, it will follow you, and it will be detrimental to your mental health and your future relationships.

Inherited Hurt

It's apparent that our parents, our grandparents, and our ancestors had their own share of trauma that they never healed from. We owe it to our children, our children's children, and future generations to pass down to them not just generational wealth but generational health. Whatever your family's particular dynamic is, be aware that, as children, we don't always understand our parents' history, so we take on what we perceive to be their truths. Our parents didn't understand their parents, so they took on their truths, pain, and traditions. For so long, we have inherited our ancestors' pain, hurt, and brokenness because a lot of us are too afraid to face our past, our mistakes, our hurts, and our brokenness, and so we've allowed ourselves and our children to go through life in emotional torment and psychological chaos. We've been so afraid of not being the loving parent, the hero mom or the hero dad, that we play victim and the good guy to mask our own damage and brokenness. To help break the cycle of inherited hurt, it is crucial to be honest with your children about your truth instead of letting them create their own hurtful conclusions about your story.

Unmindful Patterns

One thing that makes every single one of us unique is how we each interpret our experiences. We may share similar feelings, views, concerns, traditions, and even history, but every experience is processed differently. We were all created with the same basic functions (despite genetic and environmental differences) to breathe, to see, to hear, to smell, to feel, to learn, to grow, to experience, to create memories, to serve our purpose.

Somewhere along the way, we start forming our own patterns, our traditions, our cultures. We form our opinions of what's normal and what's not, what's true and what isn't, what's real and what's not, what's beautiful and what's ugly. We determine our generational patterns based on our last names, financial status, social and economic quarrels, hatred, love, and biases.

If you grow up a racist household, chances are you will become a racist. Similarly, if you grow up in a household where everybody yells and screams at each other, that too will be your way of communicating. Generational patterns are continuously and unwittingly passed down from parents to their children; and we carry those patterns into our adulthood, our relationships, and communities. Being unmindful of our behavioral patterns and blind spots will hinder our emotional growth and healing process.

CHAPTER 9

NO REALLY, IT'S NOT YOU, IT'S ME

ALTHOUGH YOU DON'T ALWAYS HAVE control over what people do or say, taking accountability for how they make you feel is your responsibility. It's not that you are blaming yourself for their actions, or being invulnerable to hurtful behavior or words, especially from the people you love dearly—but not taking responsibility for yourself and your emotions will affect your peace of mind and deter you from your purpose. When you reach emotional maturity and take responsibility for how and what you allow to affect you, your response to things that would enrage you in the past becomes lighter and more graceful; your behavior to negativity becomes purposefully nourishing and no longer damaging. As I've gotten wiser, more grounded in my purpose and my well-being, I've realized a lot of the things that have happened in my life occurred because of who I was and where I was emotionally. I often lost sight of who I was meant to be and my self-worth. I didn't know who I was; I was broken, confused, lost, and searching for love in all the people who had no healthy love to share.

Then one day, I realized that my lack of self-worth was an indication of all the unresolved traumatic experiences, the detrimental behavior I found acceptable, and how much of myself I was willing to sacrifice for the sake of what I hoped to gain from those people. I was searching for others, situations, and materialistic possessions to fill up my empty cup. This led me to be mistreated and continuously disregarded, which was destructive to my self-esteem and to my mental health. I've since learned to take accountability and stop blaming others for their unhealthy behaviors. I can't control how others behave, nor can I raise them to be better or to heal themselves, but I can teach them how to treat me by how I treat myself and what I choose to accept from them. We teach people how to treat us.

I understand that sometimes you may find yourself in situations where you feel like you have no other option but to allow whatever that's happening to happen. I remember a good friend in high school, who was kind, sensitive, caring, and loving; she was an all-around beautiful soul. She was dating a man who was a few years older than she was, so he had already graduated high school and was living a different life than she was. She told me she had plans to go college and earn her bachelor's degree, have a career, and build a better life for herself and those around her. But soon after she graduated, however, she became pregnant and college was no longer an option. Her relationship became abusive and before she knew it, years had gone by and her choice to leave became slimmer and slimmer. As a friend who had never been in her situation, or experienced what she was going through, I didn't know how to help her; I struggled with the idea of why she didn't just leave him. I advised her to move, get the help of family members, but she never had the courage to. The point is, when you allow yourself to get to a place of brokenness, where others have control over your well-being, this beautiful gift of life that you were blessed with is no longer yours.

I know leaving a situation, a job, a relationship that's mentally and physically damaging can be the hardest thing to do, especially when you're mentally broken and physically drained; but in order to find healing and live a purposeful life, you have to be courageous enough to prioritize your health and peace of mind. Others will treat you based on how you treat yourself and your gifts, mind, body, and soul. If you invite guests to your clean, spotless house, they'll treat it with the same respect that you gave it. But if your house looks like a dump, they'll treat it just like you do. It's the same for how people treat us. If I speak respectfully, act reverently towards myself and others, people will treat me with equal respect. When you respect and take care of your gifts, others will learn to do the same, because you won't tolerate anything less.

If someone disrespects or mistreats you one time and you decide to let them get away with it, don't make excuses if it happens again. You've taught them that it's okay to treat you that way. Instead, you must teach others how to treat you. When I first moved to New York from Boston, trying to start a new life, I was broke, alone, and feeling sorry for myself; my confidence level was low. I was a young fitness trainer working with a well-off, middle-aged client. I was new to the profession. One day he started raising his voice at me, behaving like I was beneath him. I am a polite, kind, calm guy, always have been, and I barely raise my voice even when I'm upset. I stayed calm and let him finish throwing his tantrum. At the end of the session, I asked him, "How are you feeling?" He said, "Fine." I said, "Okay, have a great day, I'll see you on Thursday," which was two days later.

I kept replaying the incident in my head, analyzing it, and trying to understand why he acted that way. I said to myself, maybe he was having a bad day. Ten minutes into our next session, the same behavior started again. I thought, this guy is really trying to belittle me. I stopped the session and suggested, "Can we chat outside for a bit?" I started walking out and he followed me. As we got to the stairs outside the gym, I asked him if everything was okay. Again he replied that everything was fine. I said, "Actually, everything's not fine. You're paying me to render a service to you. I treat you with the utmost respect. I am professional. I provide outstanding services and I demand the same courtesy in return. This is the second time you've started talking to me like a child, as if I'm beneath you. Are you aware of that?"

He said, "No, I'm not." I said, "Well, if this happens again, I will gladly refund your money and we can go our separate ways." Suddenly he started getting defensive. I said politely again, "I don't really understand your frustrations. But I respect that you feel frustrated and feel the need to express yourself that way. Let's cut the session short and I will leave you a check for the remaining sessions later today."

I walked away; so did he. He was in disbelief, pissed off. I assumed that no one had ever talked to him that way. A week later, he called. He said, "Mark, I really want to apologize for my behavior. I wasn't aware that I was acting that way, I'm truly sorry." I had taught him how I wanted to be treated, so he learned to acknowledge how to treat me and apologize for his behavior. I wasn't mean, I wasn't rude, I wasn't tough; I just taught him how I should be treated. I accepted his apology, and he remained my client for years. We cracked jokes together, we talked politics, religion, relationships, you name it.

Whether you're starting a new relationship, a friendship, or a professional relationship, if someone refuses to treat you how you ought to be treated, call them out or walk away.

Don't Make It For You

As Christians and believers, we pray to God, asking him to give us what we want; and although we may say, "Thy will be done," if it's not what we were expecting, we are disappointed. I can attest to this. Have you ever gotten into relationships with people you had no business being with? Or find yourself being around people that drain you mentally, spiritually, and emotionally, just because you want them to be for you? You forced, you fought, you convinced, you persuaded, you insisted, just to end up with nothing but heartaches and brokenness in the end? Sometimes we justify and redefine negative behavior just to get what we want. We make excuses, hoping the people who disappoint us will change, and that things will get better. We rationalize bad behavior, we blame ourselves, and we ignore signs that existed in former failed relationships because of our wants. But when something or someone is for you, you won't need to "work" for them.

I've seen people spend so much energy working to get into committed relationships with people who reject them in so many ways. People will intentionally make life, and loving difficult, just to see how hard someone will work to have them. That's just gruesome and unhealthy. The fact is, if you have to work to get somebody's love or get into a relationship with them, you will need to work twice as hard to maintain and keep that love and relationship. But some of you are probably wondering what's wrong with that. After all, that's what society teaches; you work hard for what you want, and if it comes easy, then it's not worth it. However, sharing your gift of love and life with someone should not feel like work. It should not feel draining and you definitely shouldn't have to beg someone to share their gifts with you, nor should you feel like you have to beg them to share yours with them. We force ourselves into miserable relationships, friendships, and situations that, if we valued ourselves enough, we would have never gotten into. We work ourselves to death for companies that have no interest in our values, our health, our well-being, our purpose, or even our lives. We sacrifice our peace of mind for people who never valued it in the first place. It's time to take control of you. You can spend all your life doing what's right for everyone else—but until you start doing what's right for you, you will never be at peace with yourself.

Distancing Toxicity

Folks who are so afraid of not being heard and understood will climb mountains so they can speak their minds. They'll dismiss others' points of view and even reword others' ideas just to find something to say. Being able to identify toxic people before sharing your gifts with them is critical. Understanding who is truly detrimental to your well-being will save you, your relationships, and even your life.

Some people find pleasure in disagreements, in chaos, in creating hurtful situations, because they are holding on to hurt, pain, and disappointment. They are hurting so badly that they find comfort in hurting others. Something is missing in their lives and only they can fill that void. It is not your responsibility to carry their pain, although you can help them identify ways to find healing. Remember, your self-care, your healing, your peace of mind, and your gifts are your priority.

Communication Red Flags

If someone tells you, "I'm right and you're wrong," it's not a conversation you want to continue. That person is essentially saying, "I don't value what you have to say, I don't want to hear your opinion, I know better than you." And if someone continuously cuts you off just so they can get their point across, you do not want to continue that conversation. Bruce Lee said it best: "Do not correct a fool or he will hate you; correct a wise man and he will appreciate you." People won't change their habits or their bad learned behaviors until they see a reason to do so, or unless they are willing to acknowledge, admit, and accept that change is needed.

I value peace of mind. I don't need to be right, because I'm always open to learning. I don't need to convince you to see my point if you are committed to misunderstanding me. I'm not going to make you see otherwise unless you're open to hearing my opinion. I know when to let go and when to be persistent. You don't need to give others a piece of your mind if it means losing your peace of mind. The person who is ready to hear and understand you won't need you to put up a fight, or fight with you just to get your point across. I'd rather put my energy into something or someone that uplifts me. Fighting will drain you, whether it is what you are used to or not. Fighting will make you physically and emotionally sick. Some people will make life difficult, chaotic, and unbearable because they're consumed by fighting, and pushing their agenda on others. They are hurting and need healing. Internally, they are living in turmoil, fighting themselves. Again, you are responsible for your well-being. Remain in control of your life and your greater purpose.

Taking Accountability

We all have what I like to call "unfavorable human moments," whether it's anger, aggression, or frustration. It's your innate right to have them. But you should understand that your human moments are your responsibility alone. You are in charge of your emotions, your behaviors, what you say, how you react to circumstances, how you allow things to affect you, physically and emotionally; it's all your choice. People also have the right to react to your human moments as they see fit. I often hear people say that you can't tell someone how to express their hurt. Of course I can! I can't tell you how to feel, but if expressing your hurt means hurting me or hurting other people, yes, I can. As adults, we are responsible for all our actions—period. As long as you're psychologically well balanced and cognizant of your behaviors, you are responsible for your actions as well as your reactions. Until you take accountability, you'll find yourself in predicaments that require you to either blame others or be victimized.

Taking accountability means admitting your actions affect others in a negative way. It means being vulnerable; it means putting aside your pride; it means humbling yourself to someone other than God; it means valuing someone else's feelings; it means saving your relationships and your friendships. Admitting you've been or done wrong doesn't make you a bad person. I realize that many of us refuse to be wrong because we associate our actions with our character. If we admit to doing something harmful that hurts others, we feel it makes us a bad person. But it doesn't. We are humans who are in pain, we will make mistakes, we will hurt others, consciously or subconsciously. People will be hurt by our actions whether we meant to hurt them or not. You don't have to live your life apologetically, but acknowledging when your actions hurt others only makes you a better person.

Accountability Is Not Blaming

Blaming others and not assuming accountability for your actions will deter your healing process. Not acknowledging or admitting that your actions can be hurtful and damaging to others will prevent you from accepting the unhealthy patterns you need to confront in order to grow and reach your purpose and live a healthier life. Accountability is not self-blame. Taking accountability comes with emotional and spiritual maturity. Accountability means acknowledging and being aware of your own actions; blaming means you may or may not be at fault.

We may not like to admit when we're wrong because it makes us feel vulnerable, especially if we've been chastised in the past. I've been there. I've made excuses to justify hurting those I loved most because I wasn't proud of my actions. I've also made excuses because I wanted others to take accountability for their actions before I could hold myself accountable for my own. But when I started taking accountability for my wrongdoings, I started being at peace with myself. I stopped blaming myself for other people's negative behaviors. By holding myself accountable for what I do, how I act, and how I treat others, I became more productive, more empathetic, kinder, and more genuine with my self-worth. What you don't do to hurt yourself, you won't do to hurt someone else. As you embark on your healing journey, keep in mind that besides what God intended for you, you are in control of how you choose to live your life. You are in control of your healing process; own it, accept it, and embrace every aspect of it.

The Problem. The Solution

The hardest thing for most of us to accept is admitting that we could be part of the problem. We go generation after generation blaming others because we truly believe that we can do no wrong. You may not be the cause of the problem but the fact that you tolerate it, the fact that you accept it year after year, makes you part of the problem. In order to grow and build healthier and more fulfilling lives, we have to stop pointing fingers and playing innocent, stop playing the victim, because the truth is we're all broken and need healing. We are all hurting and need to ease the pain. We carry the dysfunction of slavery, our parents, our friends, society, our past relationships, our hurtful experiences; we are the problem, so let's find the solution.

And if you feel you're not part of the problem or become offended by learning that you may be, you're far deeper into denial and may be causing more problems, hurt, and pain than you are aware of. If you're not ready and willing to look at yourself, to look at your history, to look at whoever raised you, to look at your experiences, to look at your friends, to look at your past and present relationships, you are the problem, because you're not ready to let go of all the things that may be causing chaos. I know because I too have been the problem; I've hurt people because of the way I loved them—with my pain, my ego, my sadness, my selfishness, my hurt, my traumas, and my chaos. I was the problem for putting up with other people's chaos and detrimental habits for years and thinking that it was normal. I've made excuses for people's behavior because I didn't know how to value myself. Because I didn't think I was enough, I tolerated everything that destroyed my mental and emotional well-being. And because I was used to chaos and dysfunction, I thought it was normal. I may not have known better, but it didn't make me less part of the problem. I am the problem when I think I no longer need to grow and improve myself. I am the problem when I blame everyone and never hold myself accountable.

We can go around looking for ways to empower ourselves, but until we take responsibility for our share of the problem, until we learn our history and find healing from our brokenness and open wounds, until we change that defective mindset, we'll keep multiplying the problem. When we keep searching for others to complete the love that we have or don't have for ourselves, we'll continue to love with our brokenness, our pain, our jealousies, our insecurities and suffering. We'll continue to find ourselves in unfulfilling and contentious relationships and still think it's normal. We all have some healing to do, and we can find the solution through purposeful living and self-reflections.

CHAPTER 10

HEALING

NO DOUBT, MOST OF US have something we need to heal from. Some hurt, some disappointment, some traumatic experience, some scar, shamelessness, some guilt, some fear. Every now and then something creeps into our mind that makes us feel inadequate, unimportant, less than, not enough, unloved, not belonging, small, anxious, depressed, and empty. Some of you may be wondering, "What do I need to heal from?" If you made it this far, you probably understand the process and the conscious decision it requires in order to find healing and live in your purpose. When we're feeling physically sick, we go see a medical doctor to find out what's wrong. We go to church, some of us, to heal our spirit and nourish our soul. But where do we go to heal our mind, our emotional and psychological health? How many of us are actually aware of our mental health and make conscious decisions to talk to a therapist or a mental health professional?

Many of us have been suffering for so long, we no longer think of it as a crisis. Some of us were born into mental anguish, which feels perfectly normal. Your learned habits may be preventing you from going through your healing process. What have you done to break the detrimental patterns that keep disrupting your peace of mind, your joy, your life? Most of your friends and family love you the way you are and are perfectly okay with you being the way you are because it benefits their dysfunctional patterns. Some of your friends would rather talk about you behind your back with your other friends instead of being honest with you. Whom are you relying on to tell you the truth if you're not honest with you? In order to find healing and live in your purpose, you must reflect on how you can be healthier.

You have to be open to criticism, suggestions, and guidance from those you trust most, from those with wisdom, from those who have learned from their own shortcomings and became healthier. This doesn't mean you'll start doing what everybody else wants you to do. On the contrary, it means you'll be open to look at the man or woman in the mirror in order to see yourself a little clearer.

Sometimes we're so busy guarding and protecting ourselves, we're quick to snap at anyone who notices our dysfunction. We can be so protective and defensive of our bad habits; we block every blessing that was meant for us. But healing, similar to salvation, is a personal journey—it is for you. It means living a healthier and a more purposeful life. It means living a less emotionally and spiritually exhausting life, one where you won't be constantly fighting with your conscience and the outside world. Healing is the ability to be open to unselfish love. Healing is embracing inner peace that no one else can touch. Healing is not stopping to throw rocks at every dog that barks at you. Healing is knowing what deserves a silent or a verbal response. Healing is for you to be able to have healthy relationships with your children, your parents, your friends, your co-workers, your neighbors, and your spouse and partner. Healing is becoming a more purposeful, healthier being.

The Process

In the process of healing yourself, you may heal someone who didn't think he or she would ever find healing. It won't be an easy journey, but you owe it to yourself to live the life you were born to live. Healing comes in different forms. It may be a conversation with your parents, if you still have them, to get clarity. It may be taking a break to replenish your mind and spirit. It may be self-forgiveness so you can get rid of that heavy burden you've carried in your heart for so long. It may be creating closure for losses that left doors unshut with unanswered questions.

Sam, a sixty-three-year-old client, told me he hadn't spoken to his son for over ten years. He said he didn't deserve forgiveness because he felt like he had abandoned his son. He blamed himself for not having a relationship with him, because he didn't know how to have a relationship with his children when he and his wife got divorced. For years he beat himself up for not putting more effort into getting shared custody of his two children. Although his daughter forgave him and understood why it wasn't healthy for her parents to stay together, the guilt and remorse of not being part of their lives destroyed him emotionally and spiritually. When he found out he was diagnosed with brain cancer, he convinced himself that he deserved to have cancer as payback for his mistakes of not being a good father. When his daughter informed her brother of their father's diagnosis, the son agreed to see him.

As difficult as it may have been for him and his son to have a conversation and find healing, they extended grace to one another and forgave. Sam ended up beating cancer and he and his son now have a great relationship. Sometimes it takes a tragedy to create healing; sometimes it takes the death of a loved one to realize that life is not worth all the fights, pain, and hurts. The truth is, until you understand your purpose, learn to be healed, and become emotionally, spiritually, and psychologically well rounded, you can't create wholesome relationships.

A friend told me how frightened she was by the idea of allowing herself to be vulnerable in her relationships. I understood why she felt afraid of giving another person so much power over her, because the way most of us love one another is painful. Loving someone is scary when it's unhealthy, but it can be beautiful when it is done in a healthy, loving, and sacrificial way. I don't think we often understand what it means to be responsible for another person's love, soul, heart, and body when they choose to share them with us. So I learned loving others is not about giving your gift to someone else; it's about sharing it.

Share, Don't Give

The idea of giving yourself to someone is petrifying. You might wonder, if I give myself to someone, does that mean I no longer own myself? Does it mean that this person can do whatever they please with me? The mistake that most of us make is that we give too much of ourselves. We overshare and overextend ourselves in the name of love and ultimately end up finding ourselves empty, broken, and lost after others decide they no longer have use for us.

When you get into a relationship, you shouldn't *give* yourself to that person; you should *share* yourself with that person. A lot of us end up being taken for granted by our loved ones and those closest to us because they feel like we are theirs to do whatever they want with. Some people will intentionally destroy you mentally, spiritually, and physically if you allow them to. They'll strip you naked psychologically and empty you out emotionally. So don't be afraid to take your gift away from them. Unhealthy love is scary.

This is why knowing who you are and who you were meant to be—*before* you decide to share your gifts with someone else—is so important. It is why you must share and not give. When you know who you are, when you know what you bring to the table, when you know your purpose, when you have enough love to share and know when to stop sharing, when you understand how to set boundaries, when you know what you will and will not tolerate, when you value your peace of mind, when you value your growth and worth, when you understand what your journey requires, when you are healed, you are ready to share your life.

But choosing someone to share your life with is only half the battle. As important as it is to have a companion or a mate, accumulating enough love for yourself will prevent you from choosing people out of despair and loneliness. It will prevent you from remaining hopeful in hopeless relationships and environments that are only tearing you down. Take your time and heal and become who you were meant to be, and you will attract people who will help fuel your journey as much as you will fuel theirs. When you are healed and ready to share your gifts, you will both understand that being with each other doesn't mean that you own one another; you can appreciate and cherish each other. You won't take each other for granted because you'll understand that every moment you share together is a gift. You will understand that the purpose of being in each other's lives is not just to be with each other but rather to help one another continue to heal and to help each other live in your purpose. It's to fuel each other's engine in order to have enough power and will to make it to your destination when you are running on empty.

Whomever you choose to share your gifts with shouldn't destroy them even though they have the power to. They shouldn't toss them around because they're not having a good day. Your gifts shouldn't be seen as a burden. That person should be there to improve and enhance your precious gifts.

Failing In Love

Many people are missing out on fulfilling relationships and purposeful love because they're hanging on for dear life to the idea of what being romantic should look like and what someone should do for them. But I get it. It's been sold that way in Hollywood, novels, and the media. We have an illusion of what love is supposed to look like. We were all born to love and be loved. There's a reason why we cry when we watch "romantic" movies or television shows, or when we read a love story with a happy or sad ending. We all want to feel loved; we all want to experience that deep connection with someone. Unfortunately, some of us believe that if love doesn't feel or look a certain way, then it's not real love. If it doesn't give you butterflies and make you see rainbows, then it's not real. Some of us have been sold on the idea of an objectified, materialized, and selfish love instead of the sacrificial, innate love that we all possess. Many of us have no idea what the meaning of love truly is and how we're supposed to personally feel if we were to ever find it.

We have no knowledge of how to love ourselves, because we grew up in a chaotic and dysfunctional home. We have been taught to see love with what we can see, with what we can get, and by how much we can gain from it. Many have been convinced to search for that Prince Charming or beautiful princess who will make their hearts skip a beat. We have been taught to value beauty over quality, strength over gentleness, meanness over kindness. But in order to find inner healing and create that deep connection with another soul, we must understand the meaning of having a companion, a partner, a support system, and sacrificial love. We must relinquish the notion of romanticism and start understanding the real characteristics of love. If romance is your priority, you need to create it by acknowledging and accepting the sacrifices that your partner makes for you. So many of us treat our loved one poorly and expect to receive the world from him or her, in the name of how much we deserve. You cannot demand someone to love you the way you want him or her to love you, especially if you don't even know how to love yourself; only you can love yourself the way you want to be loved, if and when you know how.

When it comes to love, we practice what was modeled to us by our parents and what society teaches. Some of us know how to be soft, vulnerable, affectionate, loving, kind, grateful, and attentive when it comes to our kids, but not with a partner. Our parents weren't always grateful for one another. We need a shift in our romantic mindset, in the way we love, if we want to create healthy and loving relationships.

We must learn to appreciate the person who chooses to share their love and gifts with us and appreciate the fact that they appreciate and cherish us sharing ours with them. We have to start focusing on the things that actually bring closeness and oneness between us. The acts of sharing, respecting, sacrificing, helping, healing, caring, supporting, listening, appreciating, kindness, thoughtfulness, creating and building memories together—those are the things that will create lifelong bonds. Anyone can learn to play the romantic and say everything you want to hear, especially if they want to get something from you. Anyone with wealth can buy you everything you desire. But truth is, none of that will create lasting and fulfilling relationships.

Love Anxiety

I saw a video clip of a woman running over her partner with a car after discovering that he had been unfaithful. I know this is disturbing to visualize. The fact that someone can get to the point of taking someone else's life shows how painful and unhealthy relationships can be when we're broken, empty and have little to no healthy awareness of our own gift of life and others'. Because when you love and value your gifts, you will always prioritize their purpose. If you decide you no longer want to share your life with someone, that's your right. And if someone decides they no longer want to share their gifts with you, that's his or her right as well. But because of love anxiety, we expect someone we love and share our gift with to become our property, our possession. In this woman's case, she must have felt like her gift had been shattered. She must have felt like that man's gift also belonged to her and the only thing to do was to destroy it. "Hurt people hurt people" is real. When you allow yourself to get to a place of brokenness, you no longer own your gift, because your pain and hurt can take it all away in an instant.

If you're sharing your gift with others and they no longer value and respect it, wish them well and let them go. Take your gift back; hold on to it, polish it, clean it up, embellish it, and heal your gift. The longer you allow them to misuse and mistreat it, the longer it will take you to reclaim your life. There's no need to throw away your own gift by destroying someone else's. People with love anxiety might feel the need to control their loved one just to make sure the person they feel entitled to remains theirs; that's torture. If your gift is not wanted, take it back; it's the one thing that you were blessed with. I'm not saying it will be easy, but being mistreated and taken for granted is not either. And if you're not ready to treat and appreciate someone else's gift, let them find someone who will; you don't own them. If you were taking their gift for granted, they have the right to take it back—it's theirs.

You have to care for your gift, protect it, and preserve it. Don't just pass it around and expect anyone to know how to treat it; cherish it instead.

Seal the Void. Fill the Emptiness

There's an old saying: If you give a homeless person a million dollars, chances are by the following week everything will be spent. This might not always be the case, but the idea is that when people are low, giving them money might not be the answer unless they're taught how to manage and multiply it. It's like Proverbs 12:10, which says: "Give a man a fish and you feed him for a day; show him how to catch a fish and you feed him for a lifetime." People who are emotionally and spiritually empty will always seek others to fill their emptiness, partly because they no longer have enough to give to themselves, or perhaps they were never taught how to do so. They may not have any emotional energy and spiritual courage left in them. Those who are takers will take. In a relationship, if a partner feels empty regardless of how much his or her partner gives, chances are something is missing in that partner's life. That void we feel when nothing seems to be enough, when we are longing for more, can only be filled by ourselves. Many of us become dependent on our spouses, on our friends, and our family members to keep our cup full. But it's not their responsibility to do so; they can't. Someone who is completely empty will take and take until you are both left empty.

The point is, as takers or givers, when you are feeling empty and broken, it is your responsibility to find healing and refill your cup. Focusing on your own self-care is about healing your past traumas and open wounds. The emptier you are, the more you'll feel the need to extend yourself and give to others; be mindful of those desires. Understand your limit. When you're empty, you may choose to be in situations because you may see how you can benefit from them, but be mindful of when you are simply trying to fill a void. Your pain can blind your judgment and cloud your reasoning and lead you down destructive paths. Being hurt can cause you to make all the wrong decisions; it can make you walk away from sacrificial love straight into brokenness, and it can also keep you in places that cause you more hurt than healing. But when you take time to heal yourself and become physically and psychologically healthier, you will expect to receive less from others. You will seal your own void and fill up your own cup when it runs low.

Letting Go Is Not Quitting

Wedding vows say, "For better or for worse, till death do us part." As I write this, I'm distraught. I have said those words. It's not something I take lightly. I truly believe that, deep down, people want to be true to their vows We are taught not to give up and that quitting is not an option. Many of us hang on so tight and by the time we slip, we no longer have the strength to catch ourselves from falling. We become even more broken and shattered. When I said those words, they meant commitment, sacrifice, growth, kindness, appreciation, respect, and love—not a life sentence of hurt, anger, impatience, and destruction. It takes emotionally healthy people to have emotionally healthy relationships. When you choose to share your gift with someone, it's because you trust that your gift is safe and secure with that person. It is because you trust that this person doesn't just see you for what he or she can get from you, but for what you give to others in this world. It's because you understand each other's purposes and choose to take that journey together. But what happens when you start feeling purposeless, empty, stuck, and in disarray? Many of us have committed to the wrong relationships and stay loyal to the wrong friends or the wrong jobs. We put aside our purpose and our healing and pour ourselves into others that only take from us until there's nothing left to be taken. Knowing when to let go is not just necessary, it's a skill that will save you a lifetime of heartaches and brokenness. Knowing when to let go of pointless arguments, detrimental friendships, toxic environments, negative emotions, and unhealthy relationships is necessary to heal.

You must also start learning to say no. NO to the things that disturb your peace of mind. NO to those negative emotions that make you feel worthless and less than. NO to those negative self-talks and thoughts that only make you feel worse about yourself. NO to friends who only remember you're alive when they need you. NO when you're on the edge and all it might take is a nudge to push you over. NO to having too much on your plate that leaves you depleted and empty. NO to the kids, your spouse, your family, your church, and everything else when you need to recharge and refill your cup. NO to detrimental and toxic relationships that only leave you broken and wounded. Learning to say no when you need time to replenish will not only benefit you but it will also benefit those who love you and value your health.

The sooner you let go of the habits and the learned behaviors that are detrimental to your peace of mind, your relationships, and your health, the sooner you'll start living a happier and more contented life.

Unlearn How You Were Taught to Love

Most of us have been taught what love is by people who had no idea what love was. We learned to love ourselves the way they loved themselves:

by being neglectful physically, mentally, emotionally, and spiritually. We learned to love others the way they loved others—by abusing, using, mistreating, and hurting them, and taking them for granted.

We whip our children because we were taught that being beaten is how we are kept in check by our masters. We take for granted the sacrifices our loved ones make for us, because we were taught that we should expect those things from those who love us. We've held those we love emotionally hostage, because we believe that they're supposed to heal us and carry our burdens. We devalue those who love us, because society tells us to see ourselves as the prize, the ultimate gift wrapped in golden papers presented by God himself. Books have taught us to focus on our love languages rather than appreciating each other's efforts and sacrifices. We've been taught to want more and need less. We've prioritized receiving material gifts over receiving the gift of each other. We overlook others' sacrifices because our expectations are higher than unclimbable mountains. We live in a society that is all about me, me, me. What can you do for me? How are you benefiting me? What's in it for me? How can you make me happy? How can I use you to get to where I want to get? What do I see in you that will help me? We have been raised to make everything so much about us that we end up being left empty and unhappy, because we are not being taught to fill our own emotional cup and to have realistic expectations.

The sooner we unlearn the destructive ways we were taught to love, the sooner we'll start allowing ourselves the freedom to experience more thoughtful, selfless, and sacrificial love, and the sooner we can find comfort in one another. When we start looking at others and their sacrifices as gifts and not our rights, we will be able to stop putting ourselves above everything and start appreciating more. Think about the mother who really wants to have a child. She wants to experience that love, that connection, that child as a gift, because it is seen as a blessing. Every one of us should be—and feel like—a gift. We should be receiving each other as gifts each day, because tomorrow can be unexpected. None of us is entitled to someone else's love, life, mind, body, and soul. None of us is owed someone else's peace of mind. Life is short. Each one of us has our destiny to fulfill, we have our purpose to live in, so choosing to share that precious gift of life that you were given, for as long as you get to have it with someone else, is a blessing. Every moment should be cherished, because none of us should wait until our loved ones die to realize that their gift of life was valuable.

Have fewer unrealistic expectations, entitlements, be less "you" centered; focus less on having your own way and find healthy ways to have an "us"-centered union. We've been taught to value others' gifts of life based on how much they can do for us, how much they can give us, and what title they bring to us. We wait until we lose that gift, until death, until sickness, until it's too late to appreciate that gift or to realize it was a gift. When you unlearn those detrimental ways, you will heal, you will be able to define love and be loved, you will appreciate and be appreciated, because you will be mentally and spiritually healthy and prepared to share healthy love.

Respect. Appreciation. Sacrifice

I often hear people say that the key to a successful relationship is communication. I disagree. I'm not saying it's not important to communicate with your partner, your friends, or your children. If you are with someone you chose to be with, communication should be the least of your problems. Often we overcommunicate the wrong things and refuse to face what causes our miscommunication— ourselves. Communication is never the issue; we are. Our bad habits, our pride and egos, our self-centeredness, our sense of entitlement, our lack of understanding, our inability to listen to receive instead of listening to respond. Our pain, our needs, our resentment, and our anger are the things that hinder our communication.

But wrong is only wrong if you understand the concept of right and wrong. As I said in previous chapters, just because you were taught something, doesn't mean that you were taught it the right way or that you're doing it the right way. Chances are if you've never learned to communicate, apart from what you observed growing up, you may be doing it wrong. Some of us grew up in households where we had to fuss, fight, and throw tantrums in order to be heard. And some of us keep everything bottled up because we weren't allowed to be heard at all. And because those learned behaviors and survival skills become part of us, until we make conscious decisions to change we'll never find anything wrong with them. It is impossible to communicate with someone you have no respect for or who has no respect for you. You may hear what one another says, but you will never listen to what each other has to say. You also cannot effectively and consistently communicate with someone you don't appreciate, because their views and their words won't really mean much to you.

We need to understand that communication is not just speaking your mind and saying how you feel. Sometimes communication is about being silent and listening. Other times, it's knowing that not everything needs to be talked about, especially if you can only see how it will benefit you. It's about knowing what to say and when to say it. Sometimes it's about a five-minute hug because you may be hurting so much that saying anything will only cause more hurt. Sometimes communication is about letting your guard down and saying, "I'm sorry." And sometimes communication is about holding hands and letting them see you.

Let's explore some other techniques that may be effective for healthy relationships. We have to start loving and seeing each other with respect, appreciation, and sacrifice. When we admire someone, we appreciate that they have value. We understand every sacrifice they make because we value them. Because some of us give out of our emptiness, we end up mistreating and belittling those whom we no longer respect and see value in. The fact is, when you respect someone, you also respect how you talk to them, how you approach them, how you treat them, and how you appreciate their time, their words, their gifts, and their generosity. You see the sacrifices they make because you understand that their time is precious, valuable, and priceless.

You don't take for granted what you appreciate. When you respect and appreciate someone, you learn not to overlook sacrifices he or she makes, because you know they're not owed to you. You don't disrespect what you admire, because to you there's too much at stake. If we are going to have healthy and lasting relationships, and live that loving and purposeful life we were created for, we need to learn how to appreciate more and expect less. We need to learn how to value and respect our gifts and others' gifts and to never take those gifts for granted, because any moment may be our last.

Self-Care

As Christians and believers, we understand that salvation is a gift and it is also personal. And the way we care for ourselves can benefit others, especially our loved ones. When we do things that are healthy for us, such as eating food that makes us feel good and gives us healthy energy, or taking part in activities that bring us joy, enhance our quality of life, make us feel whole, and give us purpose, we end up feeling better about ourselves. Our worldview changes drastically and, because we feel better, the way we treat those around us also changes. We exude kindness, contentment, peacefulness, and an array of healing energy.

When we find ourselves in hurtful situations such as breakups, loss of a loved one, or betrayal, we try to find distractions, such as partying and meaningless relationships, to avoid dealing with the pain and disappointment. But the truth is, moving forward without taking the time to heal from our pain will not only cause us more pain, but it will also cause others pain. It will create deeper confusion, push us deeper into the abyss. Finding appropriate ways to heal before we move forward is essential. Taking time to heal ourselves, figuring out why we went through that trauma, will help us with the pain and give us insight into how not to put ourselves in similar situations in the future. When we are broken, defeated, empty, our first instinct is to find someone to fix us, to help us bury our hurts and move on. It's in our human nature; we want what we want, when we want it, how we want it, and we want it now. Our pain, our ego, and loneliness push us towards more hurtful situations.

Broken can't fix broken without someone getting shattered. Don't hinder your healing process. Take time to heal. Find a therapist, a pastor, a counselor—or perhaps just take time to come to terms with your situation. And if you hurt someone, analyze why you might have hurt that person; take accountability. Perhaps you still needed to heal from something else, so now is your time. Perhaps you weren't ready for that relationship; take time to figure out why. I know it's not easy being alone, but being with another person when you are broken, or being with another broken person who is not aware of his or her brokenness, can be just as lonely and detrimental to your health. Choose your aloneness wisely. Make sure you have enough to share before you choose to share yourself with someone else. Make sure your cup is not empty before you choose to start pouring into someone else's cup. Make sure you're not expecting someone else to fill your cup for you.

Going into a relationship with an empty cup is a recipe for disaster because you will deplete the other person and drain their cup. Don't become a liability to someone else. Work on you. Love on you for however long it takes. You should build a circle that you can plug your cup from when you're running low, and understand what you need to do to replenish your cup. Make meaningful connections with friends and family, so you're not only depending on yourself. And when you get with the person you choose to share your gifts with, they'll hopefully know how to protect your gifts and handle them with care—because they'll know one day God is going to call on you or that person and you will have to give it back; only the memories will remain. Be so healed that the past hurts become lessons that needed to be learned and not be repeated. When you don't take time to heal from a broken heart, a traumatic experience, you will project past hurts on a present relationship. And remember: healing and maintaining your peace is your responsibility alone.

Do It For You

I always find it to be inexplicable when someone gets upset at someone else for something they did for themselves. For instance, if someone gets their hair done and the other partner fails to notice or pay a compliment to them, the first person might get upset or feel hurt, unloved or unnoticed. Our desire to be complimented and flattered is sometimes due to a lack of self-confidence and self-love. When you exercise and take care of your health, when you eat healthily and have more energy to get through your day, those are for *you*. Self-care is not about pleasing others; it should be done for you. Nothing you do that's good for you should be done for anybody else. But it will benefit others.

Let's go back to taking care of yourself. Let's say you eat a healthy balanced diet of fresh, plant-based foods and proteins, you exercise, you stay hydrated (not with sugary drinks or alcohol), and you don't stress yourself over every little thing; subsequently, you will be in a better mood and those closest to you will see and feel the difference. They will feel good being around you, instead of feeling depleted and drained by your negative energy. You may even inspire people around you to take better care of themselves. When you do what makes you more joyful and healthier, your body will produce endorphins (those feel-good hormones) and less cortisol (stress hormones) to put you in a better mood. The food we eat impacts how we feel. High-fat, sugary foods might taste good going down, but they will make us feel depressed, anxious, and stressed.

If you don't do what is best and healthy for you and your peace of mind, you will end up punishing everyone around you. Feel good for you, and let your good feelings flow and shine on those around you. Don't spoil your healthy feeling just because others didn't notice what you did; you did it for you. Truth is, people may not always notice what you do, but they will remember how they felt around you and your energy. Take care of *you*; let your positive energy emit love, kindness, empathy, and understanding, and make others feel like they're part of your healthy process. You may even become a catalyst for their feel-good choices.

CHAPTER 11

LIVING IN YOUR PURPOSE

MANY OF US AT SOME point in our lives struggle to understand what our true purpose in life is. We work hard to accumulate wealth, houses, cars, yachts, the shiny things and the finest things that money can buy, but yet we still feel empty. We live our lives believing in those things, believing in the messages that tell us what the true meaning of happiness is but still feel like something is missing. These things are not your purpose. Hoarding wealth, destroying and hurting others are not your purpose. We all have a gift, a calling, something that brings fulfillment to our lives, something that helps and heals others, something that brings out passion and creativity. And when you finally discover what that gift is and you're able to use it for the greater good of the universe and of others, you will know your purpose in life.

But let's dig deeper. I know you're probably wondering, what is purpose anyway? We didn't always have everything we have today, such as the material possessions that we place so much value on and the money that most of us put so much belief in; but we had each other, we had bartering and helping one another. We could only survive by serving one another (although there was greed and selfishness); we were each other's healers and helpers. Growing up in Haiti, if we didn't have something, and our neighbors had it, my grandparents would either barter or borrow it from them, and vice versa. It was great. But at some point, we wanted more so we became stingy and selfish; the less fortunate stayed less fortunate, while the more privileged continued to grab more and more. We have somehow lost sight of humanity and our purpose on earth. We've become a society that idolizes wealth. Motivational speakers tell us how ambitious we need to be. Preachers tell us how much more we need to make so our 10 percent tithe can be greater and their lifestyles can be grander. The get-rich-quick authors tell us how to leapfrog our way to riches without the healing process most of us need to go through in order to live in our purpose.

If purpose is the reason something exists, what is our purpose for being here? We come into existence; some of us live for decades, others never make it to their first birthdays. In modern culture, we have been taught to work hard, to conquer, to be ambitious, to want more, to fight more, to get what's yours, to create monetary legacies. But what many of us end up doing is destroying ourselves, and hurting others, in order to accumulate more, to buy more, to make bigger profits. We break our body and soul for the sake of owning materialistic goods that none of us can ever take with us when we leave this earth. So when you ask yourself, "What is my purpose, why do I exist?" the answer is to help and to heal one another.

I believe children understand clearly what their purpose is. If you ever ask them what they want to be when they grow up, they might say they want to be a doctor or a nurse because they heal and help people when they're sick; a firefighter to save people; a police officer to protect and help people by keeping them safe; a teacher to educate others; or a superhero to help and protect others. Children understand that the purpose of each one of us being here is to help and heal one another.

The need to be financially stable and acquire materialistic possessions starts clouding our purpose and we begin to shift away from humanity and start focusing on getting what's ours. We end up getting degree after degree, and working in meaningless jobs that rob us from our callings. We end up dying inside because we know, deep down, there's no humanistic purpose in the places and jobs we spend most of our time in. Society discourages us from taking paths that lead us to our purpose.

Think of those times when you wanted to do something that helps and heals others. Whether or not you are in a position to help and heal people emotionally, physically, or financially, if you understand the purpose of which you are serving others, your life will take on a different meaning. You will love what you do because it is being done with the truest intention and the healthiest spirit; you will be living your purpose. You will love yourself differently. When you learn to understand your purpose and realize what it is, you will find the true meaning of life—both your life and the lives of others. You will appreciate your existence and every other being for the blessings that they were meant to be, and kindness, compassion, and empathy will flow through you.

Crucifixion and Rebirth

Writing this book was challenging for me. It is difficult to be grateful for the things that go wrong, the things that hurt you and cause you pain, especially when you are struggling to find the silver lining. But sometimes those experiences are the ones needed, because God uses them to use you for his greater purpose. Had we not sinned and disobeyed God, he wouldn't have had to crucify his only begotten son for the purpose of saving us. If we didn't go through the gruesome experience of slavery and become as broken as we are today, I'd have no need to write this book. If our grandparents had known better and raised their children in an emotionally healthier way, and if subsequently our parents had raised us with a healthier mindset and less pain and brokenness, I'd probably have no reason to write this book. Had I not gone through the loss of my marriage and a toxic, mentally draining relationship, I probably wouldn't be inspired to write this book. My point is, sometimes the experiences that nearly destroy us are the ones God uses to lead us to our purpose. He uses our brokenness, and our most painful traumatic experiences as part of his plan, to reach the less fortunate because he knows we are able to get through those traumas. He uses us to help and heal the ones who need to benefit from our experiences.

It may be hard to find the silver lining when you're in pain, but those detrimental relationships may be your crucifixion; experiencing the loss of a loved one may be your crucifixion. Suffering from an illness or a near-death experience may be your crucifixion. An epidemic or a pandemic may be the crucifixion that is needed in order to stop and regain focus on your purpose. This world can sink us in so deep that we can get lost going down our broken roads, straying away from our life's mission. I was in a marriage where I felt dead mentally, emotionally, and spiritually. I was empty, broken. The sad thing about being empty is you keep scraping out of your emptiness, hoping that someone will lend a hand and toss you back a bone.

If you have people in your life who are takers, or you don't know how to open your lid and receive from others or even give back to yourself, your chances of receiving and being emotionally healthy become a dead end. In my case, facing my childhood and past traumatic experiences was my rebirth. Letting go of detrimental patterns, toxic people and relationships, was my rebirth. Reclaiming peace of mind was my rebirth. I was able to search and find myself and my purpose, which was to find internal peace and self-worthiness and eventually write this book. You may be in a similar situation right now, or perhaps you may end up in one, but one thing to keep in mind is that there's a greater purpose behind your pain. What you do with it is up to you. Your rebirth may be the end of a relationship or a friendship; it may be distancing yourself from emotionally, spiritually, and physically draining people, situations, a job, or a family member. It may be learning to give up control and live life, intentionally. There will be plenty of opportunities to be rebirthed; but understanding everything we talked about when it comes to healing, letting go, and saying NO will play a pivotal role in your rebirthing process. You have the chance to be rebirthed after your crucifixion.

During my healing process, I didn't want to listen to motivational speeches telling me to reach deeper and dig deeper and push harder—because when you're broken, the deeper you go, the more pain you find and the emptier that hole becomes. So I knew I needed to heal; I knew I needed to find my purpose and understand why I was so lost and wounded. I needed to figure out what I was put here for and how I was going to use my gifts to help and heal myself and others. I was inspired to write a book that was going to help myself and others; I wanted you and me to find healing, purpose, and our reasons to be here. I wanted us to be our own source of empowerment, instead of constantly needing to recharge empowerment through our spouses, our friends, casual encounters, meaningless connections, and instant gratifications. So when you find yourself in a detrimental situation and you feel stuck, lost, and dead, know when you've been crucified and need to be rebirthed, instead of waiting to be buried and decayed. Many of us never come back from those mental, spiritual, and emotional crucifixions. We can get so lost and empty we end up burying our own selves, whether it's with work, violence, abuse, affairs, promiscuity, substances, drugs and alcohol, and even food. Knowing and understanding your crucifixion will help you take necessary steps towards your rebirth and your purpose.

Too Little, Too Much

We are constantly being told to do more, push harder, dream bigger, work harder, go further. Your body can handle anything; all you have to do is set your mind to it. People realize that we are so low on fuel and running on empty that they'll sell us anything to make us feel alive while they constantly benefit from our depletion. I truly believe we were not created merely to be destroyed by our own egos and selfish ambitions. It always puzzles me when older people tell me getting old is not for wimps. The joint and muscle aches and illnesses may have a lot to do with how they did or didn't take care of their minds and bodies in their younger years. I am also puzzled at seeing young people destroy themselves physically and psychologically by pushing the limit, driving themselves to the edge by going harder, pushing more—the "all or nothing" attitude. The number one purpose of our existence is to take care of ourselves, to become healthier, kinder, more helpful to one another, and to guide future generations to be their best and healthiest. If you're unhealthy, in pain, in agony, distress, dealing with anxiety, or feeling chronically depressed, it's hard to give your best to yourself and others.

It pains me when I hear motivational speakers urging people to push harder, give more, do more, and strive for more, without any consideration for their emotional, physical, and psychological well-being. Understand the concept of too much of a good thing. Even water, which is vital for our well-being, can become harmful when we consume too much of it; maintaining a healthy balance in everything is key. The concept of "more" in itself is a lack of satisfaction of oneself. The more you want, the less grateful you will be for what you have. The goal is not wanting more, it's wanting healthier.

Many of us reject the idea of living a balanced life because we believe more is better. And because of this, we end up accruing more pain, more hurt. When we tell ourselves we can handle more, do more, push a little harder, or last a bit longer, we find ourselves broken and unable to execute more. Like the concept of right and wrong, having too little or doing too little is synonymous to having or doing too much. If you don't take care of yourself, you pose the risk of getting lifestyle diseases, and if you become obsessed with doing more and more, you can break yourself down psychologically and physically. The concept of balance, when it comes to living in your purpose, must be understood. Knowing when to give and when to take are both important. Sharing more than what you have will be detrimental to your health and your calling, and not being able to compartmentalize your self-love and your love for your children, your spouse, and your friends and families, will leave you empty and in constant need of replenishment because you'll be giving to everyone from just one fountain.

But when you are ready to live in your purpose, you will be aware of when it is time for you to take a break, to share less, and to restock before running empty. When you are healed and ready, you will understand taking too much and hoarding too much is just as unhealthy and selfish as giving too much just to find yourself feeling depleted and empty. Wherever you are in your life's journey, maintaining a healthy balance will help you live a less damaging and selfish life.

Navigating Your Purpose

Many of us are living in our purpose even when we're not conscious of our actions; we're kind to ourselves, we help and heal others. We love and appreciate others and their sacrifices, but not being aware of it can be costly to you and those around you. If you are someone who is always ready to help others without reciprocation, you are fulfilling a purpose greater than yourself. If you focus on healing others without any return on that investment, you are also living in your purpose. But there are issues with living in your purpose when you're not ready to do so. If you're not aware that you are actually living in your purpose and doing so within healthy and constructive boundaries, you will be hurt, you will be disappointed, you will be taken advantage of, and you will continue to get broken until you realize that people are only draining your fountain.

When you only give to others and neglect yourself in the process, you are unfortunately creating more harm than good, not just to yourself but to those closest to you. As I said, a lot of us do great things, amazing acts of kindness with the right intention but the wrong spirit. When you are hurting and in pain, you become a liability to yourself, to your loved ones, and to society. You will be fragile, insecure, unsatisfied, unteachable, quick tempered, aggressive, angry, and empty, because you feel like you always have to defend yourself from people who don't even intend to hurt you.

Take the following steps to truly and wonderfully live in your purpose:

Heal spiritually, physically and psychologically. If you are hurting, it will be extremely difficult to share your healthiest self with others and still have enough left for yourself.

Become whole. A lot of us are still picking up broken pieces from our childhood traumas and past experiences. We are being driven and motivated by hurt and resentments and selfish ambitions. Until you're able to find healing for yourself and put those shattered pieces back together, the spirit in which you serve your purpose won't serve you and others.

Understand your purpose. The basis of rejecting fears and frustrations of unfamiliarity and the unknown is through understanding what is at hand. When you get to recognize your purpose, you will undoubtedly understand your visions, you will embrace them, you will understand how to manage them, and they won't feel burdensome.

Your purpose can't come with expectations. If you do for others or yourself with the expectations of receiving something in return or waiting for glorifications from others, you will be living in constant disappointment and will consequently deplete your own source of power, and your purpose will serve as detriments to your well-being.

Don't let your purpose be somebody else's dream for you. Can you remember when you were a child, before your parents and society convinced you to pursue careers that would give you financial stability instead of self-fulfillment and emotional stability? Many of us are living somebody else's dreams, visions, and purpose. We've fallen for the demands and expectations of those who live their lives vicariously through us. We've followed in our parents' footsteps and even deprived ourselves of mental stability so we could make our parents proud.

Your purpose has to be yours and it has to be what you were called to do. It may not be fancy or have a highly regarded title. It may not be glorious and celebrated, but it has to be yours and it has to fulfill your life and soul. But for any part of your purpose to start coming to fruition, you have to heal first. And whatever it is that you need to heal from, you must recognize that you need and deserve to be healed. God didn't intend for us to live broken and dysfunctional lives. He heals the brokenhearted and binds up their wounds (Psalm 147:3).

Be the Messenger, Not the Savior

In the book of Jeremiah 1:5, the scripture says: "Before I formed you in the womb, I knew you, and before you were born, I consecrated you; I appointed you a prophet to the nations." Part of our purpose as helpers and healers is to be used as vessels for those who are in need. We are appointed messengers for those who are open, ready, and willing to hear our message and share our gifts. We are helpers and healers for those who understand that they're hurting and ready to seek healing.

But in our quest to answer our calling, many of us end up getting lost in the process and stray from that calling. We start operating as if we were God the Messiah himself, and we focus on preaching to everyone else while missing our own sermons. We take it personally when people fail to receive our message because we see it as a rejection, and our ego and pride get wounded, so we condemn those who fail to accept our help. But remember, even Jesus, who was the Savior himself, never tried to convince people they needed healing; and he still got crucified. Just like salvation, healing is a personal choice that each and every one of us needs to make for ourselves. We also need to remember that we are not saviors. Some of us lose ourselves, trying to save people who are either not ready or don't want to be saved. We've opened up our sources without setting up boundaries and allow people who are not ready to accept healing to drain us, because our self-seeking ambition makes us believe that it is our job to fill up their empty cups and put their shattered pieces back together. So we end up just as broken and empty as they are. Fixing others and carrying their burdens is not your purpose. If your purpose takes away from your healing and your peace of mind, it is not your calling. Your purpose will satisfy your life; it will enhance your growth and allow you to be the helper and healer you're supposed to be without taking away from your own healing journey.

We sometimes act like we are Jesus and take it upon ourselves to decide whether others deserve condemnation or saving. We make it about us when they don't live up to our expectations. We can't accept each other's differences because we think we are the judges of their sins. Our job is to be messengers and deliver our message through our purpose; it's to live in our truths and let our light shine so bright that it radiates onto others. It's to help those who are in need and seeking help and healing. Our purpose is to be that vessel in which help and healing is provided to those who are broken, lost, and ready to be found.

Some of us have so much hate in our hearts for our brothers and sisters that we only have space left to love God. We judge others because their sins are different from ours. We cast stones because we're too frightened to look at our own reflection. But when you are living a life that is purposeful, you won't be afraid or ashamed to face yourself and challenge your own blind spots; when you recognize your purpose, then your decisions, your actions, and how you live your life will be a testimony, a walking billboard for healthier lives, more peaceful interactions, and untiring help and healing.

Have you ever noticed the more emotionally broken you are, the more you attract other broken people? Hurt people are more susceptible to receiving advice from other hurt people because their pain resonates with each other; but it won't be healing. Disseminating a message and reaching out with our thoughts, our words, our ideas, and beliefs is easier than ever before. With the click of a button, we can reach thousands and even millions of people who have yet to heal. In one way, it's great that we can share and help others see that they are not alone in their pain. On the other hand, a lot of us who are relaying those messages are still broken, hurting, disappointed, angry, and frustrated with ourselves. I'm not saying there's anything wrong with expressing yourself and sharing your experiences—but if you don't understand yourself, your situation, or where you are, and if you don't have a vision of how you need to heal from your wounds, your goal should be first to find healing and peace of mind for yourself, and start living in your purpose before you start helping and healing others.

Purposeful Living

Imagine what life would be like if everything we do was done purposefully. If every interaction enhanced health and elevated those who are down and broken. A life where we wouldn't need to hide ourselves from one another, where we could expose our wounds and give them room to heal. I want you to ask yourself, how can you live a life that makes such a difference, a life that ignites such positivity that those around you can decide to follow suit? Are you purposefully living? When you woke up this morning, did you wake up with the purpose of making the day a healthier, happier, kinder one? When you sit down to eat that meal, do you eat with the purpose of nourishing your health, that temple? Do you drink with the purpose of healing or enriching your gifts, mind, body, and spirit?

Sometimes we can be too comfortable diving into the things that are detrimental to our health, mind, body, and spirit. We can be too comfortable diving into anger and every emotion that drags down our spirit and causes us to be mean spirited, depressed, broken, and anxious. We get too complacent gossiping about our brothers and sisters and dragging each other down, and too comfortable causing pain and hurting one another. We are too comfortable letting ourselves go, ignoring our health, treating ourselves with deprivation of love instead of with kindness, grace, and self-care. In order to live a purposeful life, your first priority, your first project, has to be to heal *you*. You have to see you, you have to elevate you, you have to love you, regardless of where you are, regardless of what you have been through, regardless of who didn't want you or told you that you weren't good enough or attractive enough. You have to find you. And when you see that person, when you find that person, whether you like them or not, you owe it to yourself to give them another chance; you owe yourself that much and more. Forgive you, be truthful to you and extend grace to you and help you heal from whatever brokenness, traumas, pain, and hurt you are suffering from. To live a purposeful life, everything you do must have a purpose because *you* have a purpose.

Purposeful Love

Deciding to get to know someone, fall in love, and share your gifts with them for the rest of your life is terrifying. Although we want to be loved, cared for, cherished, hugged, kissed, and made to feel special, the idea of not "giving" but sharing yourself with another person can still be really scary, especially when you're not fully healed. Because of our unhealthy ways of loving one another, sharing our gifts with someone—while not knowing how they'll treat those gifts—has prevented us from living a life that is filled with purposeful love and selfless commitment. Our approach to love has been distorted in so many ways, many of us don't even know what love is or never knew at all. This four-letter word, which has become such a blessing and a curse for so many, has caused emotional damage and even physical violence. Jealousy, envy, obsession, selfishness, and the idea of owning someone have all driven us to cause pain to those we claim to love and are unable to live without.

But what is the purpose of falling in love and wanting to share your life with someone? What is it about this natural part of life that has such power to make us cry, laugh, and feel complete, empty, whole, broken, and alive again? Why is it so complicated for so many of us? As you already read, my approach to having a love that is fulfilling, enjoyable, satisfying and purposeful doesn't coincide with societal expectations. Finding a love that is worth sharing without the pain, the abuse, the hurt, the fights, and the arguments, first requires healing. In order to have a healthy relationship (whether spousal or familial), everyone must be psychologically, spiritually, and emotionally healthy. You cannot bring your pain and traumas into relationships and expect others to either carry them or heal them for you; it's unhealthy, it's unfair, and it's a recipe for a life filled with more pain, disappointment, and trauma.

Before I got married, I knew I wanted a healthy marriage. I knew I wanted someone I could spend the rest of my life with, someone I would love deeply and want to share my gifts with. What I didn't know, and wasn't taught, was that it takes two healthy people to have a healthy marriage. However, what I did know, and was taught, was that marriage is work; you have to fight for it. There will be hard times and you have to stick together. When you're unhealthy and broken, everything unhealthy makes sense to you. When you're in pain, the things that can potentially bring you more pain seem inviting and appealing. Are we that desperate to find love and relationships that instead of encouraging people to find healing and emotional health, we tell them to stick to it, to fight for and work for love? So many of us put our heads down, walk on eggshells, jump through burning hoops to make our unhealthy relationships work. We fight for them, cry for them, work for them, but all the while we hold on to our unhealed and broken souls, only to be crucified and buried by our own efforts and "work." Raising our children in dysfunctional cages is not the way it was intended to be. Fighting with the ones you love doesn't create a home, it builds a cage. We deserve better, healthier. I have faith that all of us can heal and create healthier selves, more loving households, and healthier, more productive communities. We can heal ourselves, help each other to find healing, and discover our purpose.

I remember writing these questions down when I was younger and used to write poetry. I had so much fear about love and relationships, watching people living in chaos and emotional distress, I knew I didn't want to be that guy—the one who abused his wife, neglected and mistreated his children. I knew I didn't want to be that guy whom his partner complains about and who never seems to be able to meet her expectations. I tried not to be that guy. And even though I didn't become that guy, I learned that relationships are not about working for it, fighting for it, or sticking it together when you're broken and only breaking each other daily.

It's not about who's the leader of the household if you were never taught what being a leader or a follower was. It's not about communicating, when the way you learned to communicate was harmful. It's not about fighting for it, when all you witnessed growing up was fighting and arguing. It's not about sticking it together, when doing so only breaks you down and derails you from living a worthwhile life. It's about recognizing that you have to heal before you have nothing but hurt to share with someone. It's about appreciating your gifts of mind, body, and soul—and the gifts of those who share theirs with you. It's about respecting and preserving the sacrifices you make for others and the ones that are made for you. It's about building a life that propels and exudes purpose and kindness, peace of mind and fulfillment. It's about joining forces to raise healthy, purposeful generations; it's about sacrificial love and common God-intended purposes.

Starting Our Purposeful Journey

The following are some questions to ask yourself before you embark on your purposeful relationship journey.

Are they ready to share their gifts with me?

You'd be surprised how many of us go into relationships knowingly and unknowingly broken, hoping to find healing through the other person. Before you take that relationship journey, you should do the following:

- Make sure you are healed and ready to grow with someone else and that they too are healed and ready to grow with you. Someone can be ready to share their life, but are they ready to share it with you? You don't want to be a spot holder or just a "for now" someone in somebody's plan. Some of us want relationships but we don't want the growth; we want our partner to accept us for who we are, whom our mother and or father taught us to be, and we are not willing to go through the process of healing, let alone growing and prospering.
- We must be responsible for ourselves and we must make sure that whomever we are embarking with on that life journey are also responsible for themselves and their gifts, finances, goals, behavior, family, and friends; we must see ourselves as part of the other person's responsibility, goals, and journey. We shouldn't go into relationships with the expectation of changing people into whom we want them to be for us. We

can't change their goals into our goals; if they understand their purpose, don't derail that.

- Make sure that your spirit is in order and that theirs is as well. One of the most detrimental things you can do to yourself is making decisions or choices with the right intention, but the wrong spirit. You can want to be healthy, you can make good choices, but if your spirit or theirs is not ready for those choices, you will ultimately cause hurt to yourself and others. Be sure to assess emotional, spiritual, and mental stability before deciding to share your gifts and before sharing someone else's.

Are they ready to commit to me?

Good people make bad choices, and bad people make good choices; that is the nature of life. Many of us can get so caught up in what we want so badly, we turn a blind eye on everything that's not good for us just to fulfill those wants. Our desire to find someone and to be with someone might cause us to cling to people who have the right intentions but the wrong spirit, even when we can see clearly that they are not ready to commit to sharing their gifts with us.

We persist, either because we want to save them or we just don't want to miss out on their good intentions. Maybe they haven't healed yet, or maybe they haven't reached their crucifixion point yet; whatever it may be, you have to make sure that they are ready to commit to you. You also have to make sure they understand what love is and what it means for both of you. You can both want a loving and fulfilling relationship, but if you don't know what a loving and fulfilling relationship looks like and feels like, you will find yourselves in emotional dismay and constant emptiness. At some point, you may get ill; there will be losses; there may even be times when finances are in turmoil. Are they ready to commit to help and mend, to repair and rebuild with you? Life will have its ups and downs. I'm not talking about the relationship, although relationships have these, too; but if you prioritize your healing, peace of mind, and purpose, the ups and downs within the relationship shouldn't be detrimental but, rather, moments to reflect on, replenish, revitalize, and heal your mental state, individually or as a unit. And when those hard times come, you need a teammate who will understand that this shouldn't pit you against one another, but rather use it as an opportunity to huddle up and strategically move forward as a team.

What kind of sacrifices are they willing to make for me?

As discussed before, love is an act of sacrifice. In the Old Testament, in order to prove one's atonement and commitment, a sacrificial act was required. Just like God sacrificed his son to save us, he expects us to repay him for his sacrificial love by the sacrificial acts that we do for one another: by appreciating, respecting, and understanding that he is God and that he made a priceless sacrifice for us. As stated in Hebrews 13:12: "Do not neglect to do good and to share what you have, for such sacrifices are pleasing to God." When we choose to share our gift of life with someone else, we don't expect to be compensated for our love and sacrifice. However, we do hope to be loved in return, appreciated for our gifts, and acknowledged for our act of sacrifice. The most meaningful way you can show your love to someone is through the sacrifices that you are ready and willing to make for him or her. As written in Romans 13:8: "Owe no one anything except to love one another, for he who loves another has fulfilled the law." We don't deserve the grace of God, but we receive it over and over again. We didn't deserve the sacrifice of his life, but we also received it. Sometimes, due to our selfish and unappreciative attitude, we don't deserve anyone's love—but we still receive it. That sacrificial love and that sacrificial commitment that we often overlook and take for granted can be the key to a fulfilling relationship and purposeful love. Be certain that whomever you want to share your gifts and build a future with understands, appreciates, and is ready for that sacrificial love and commitment. Always choose love over hate, appreciation over entitlement, and peace of mind and healing over ego and self-righteousness.

Do they appreciate and respect themselves?

In any relationship, whether it is friendship, familial, or professional, two things can make or break that bond: appreciation and respect. If there's no appreciation, then there's little to no value to that relationship, and if there's no respect, then there's no understanding, communication, and ultimately no relationship. Find someone who understands respect and unwavering appreciation for their gift of life, their peace of mind, their healing and purpose. Find someone who appreciates and respects your gifts of mind, body, and spirit, because they know tomorrow is not promised and every moment spent sharing your gifts with one another is sanctified. Find someone who appreciates and respects their emotional, physical, and spiritual health; someone who values healing over gratification, vulnerability over pride; someone who has a purpose and who's committed to making the world a healthier place by helping and healing others.

Let's face it—if people have no respect and appreciation for themselves, their life, their purpose, their visions, their health, their peace of mind, they won't respect and appreciate those attributes in you. And you don't have to feel bad for not wanting to share your gifts with them. It doesn't mean that they're bad people, it doesn't mean that you think you're better than they are; it simply means that you value and treasure your gifts too much to let someone else disrespect and take them for granted.

Are they worthy of my gifts?

When I was younger, in spite of my lack of self-worth, I knew the purpose of my gifts was far greater than my insecurities—the love I felt was missing and everything that was tearing me apart emotionally. I knew I had so much more than just myself as a boy and a man to offer to society; I knew I wanted to create opportunities and help others heal and reach their purpose. But the thing about being broken and defeated is that your lack of self-fulfillment pushes you to share your gifts with anyone who makes you feel the love you wish you had for yourself. When your cup is completely dry emotionally, anyone who pours a drop of replenishment, a drop of recognition, a drop of romance, a drop of appreciation, a drop of anything you're lacking of and craving for, makes you think they are worthy and deserve to share your gifts.

I've wasted time and energy demeaning my gifts because I was too empty to recognize who could appreciate and help my gifts blossom. I thought I could fix others when I couldn't even fix my own brokenness. I thought I could heal and save others when my own spirit was dead and needed healing and saving. I became more wounded by allowing those who weren't ready to share my gifts to have access to them. I lost pieces of my shattered self by allowing those who had no intention of sharing, but only of taking, to have access to my gifts. I lost myself by hoping to find others. I hated myself so I could love others the ways they wanted and expected to be loved; I had to learn that my gifts belong to me and not everyone is worthy of them.

Some folks can hide their brokenness so well, at first glance they'll fool you into thinking that they are God's chosen companion to your gifts. They may always know the right things to say, the right things to do; and because we can't wait to feel whole with someone, because we can't wait to cast away our loneliness, we give away our precious gifts to those unworthy of them. We get blinded by smiles, material things, beautiful words, physical appearance, and become emotionally unhealthy. Focus on loving yourself more; fill up your cup so you're not lacking self-care and self-fulfillment. Don't allow your craving for affection and attention to push you to liquidate your gifts. Make sure people are worthy of your mind, body, and spirit. Make sure they'll know how to appreciate your gift of life before you open the door and allow anyone to use your gifts as they please.

CHAPTER 12

TEACHING OUR CHILDREN

BEING A PARENT IS SUCH an enormous responsibility that sometimes I wish there was a vetting process to determine who's emotionally, physically, and spiritually ready enough to take on that role. Think about it: you are essentially in charge of guiding someone's gift of life, shaping their future, training them how to view and navigate the world around them. You are teaching them how to either make the world a healthier place or to become a liability to themselves and others. Our job as parents is vital; the psychological health of our children depends on how healthy or broken we raise them to be.

We have the responsibility to mold their lives by how we love them, care for them, and protect them, and whether we give them memories that they will either cherish or suffer from for the rest of their lives. I know we're not perfect, and we'll never be. I know a lot of us have yet to heal from our own psychological wounds. I know many of you are carrying the load of raising your children alone and it is as difficult as it is gratifying. And sadly, some of you find yourselves raising them in unhealthy, unsafe, violent, toxic, and just simply damaging ways—but still trying to do your best.

Raising well-rounded sons and daughters is the responsibility we were granted. None of those challenges exempts any of us from taking that responsibility enthusiastically. But, as parents, we must make conscious decisions to better ourselves, heal ourselves, take care of ourselves, and become the healthiest version of ourselves—if not for ourselves, then for the sake of our children. We owe it to them to be at peace. We owe it to them to make ourselves whole so they can learn to grow whole and stay whole psychologically. They deserve to have physically, emotionally, spiritually, and psychologically healthy parents and people they can look up to, model, and truly aspire to be.

As parents, many of us don't teach our children how to create a life of inner satisfaction and self-fulfillment because most of us are living unsatisfied and unfulfilled lives. Because of our fears, regrets, pain, and our emptiness, we teach them how to get by, how to go on through life without crumbling, how to fight, how to stand up for themselves, how to be strong, and how to survive, because that's all we were taught. But what we are really teaching them is how to live a life of constant disappointment, constant conflicts and chaos, constant emotional hurt, and reliving childhood traumas over and over again. We're teaching them that to live is to fight and survive. With that comes low self-esteem and expecting others to love them more than they love themselves.

As children, we model what we see in whoever raised us. If you treat your loved ones badly, you're teaching your children to do the same; if you treat strangers unkindly, you're teaching them to act the same, consciously or subconsciously. Our behavior as parents, the way we speak, and our habits, good or bad, are all lessons for our children. Your children will forget what you said to them when they were five years old, but they'll remember your actions, your mannerisms when they were two years old. They will love you regardless of what you are able to give to them financially, but they will remember the lack of your affection, the lack of emotional and psychological guidance, the lack of your values, caring ways, support, and love. If you're not healthy enough to give them those essential assets, you may miss out on having a great and healthy relationship with them. Your children need you to teach them; they need you to care even when they act like they don't; so don't fail to teach them right from wrong out of fear of losing their love and affection. It's better to teach them how much you care, by creating healthy guidelines for them to follow, than to let them do whatever they want out of fear of losing them.

Be More Than Words

In a world of political correctness, many of us are afraid to speak our mind freely because we either don't want to offend a wounded society or be "cancelled." I'm not saying it's okay to be insensitive or to be all truth and no grace with your children and others, because the words we speak have power and they sometimes last a lifetime. The key is to teach our children more so by our actions and less by our words.

Let's teach them healthy values and morals that will help them choose selflessness over selfish gratifications. Teach them the value of words by how we treat and respect ours. Teach them the value of setting up boundaries. Saying no to them is not necessarily a bad thing. In fact, you should teach your children the meaning of the word. Sometimes when God says no to your prayers, it's not because he doesn't love you or doesn't care about what you're praying for. It's because he wants to protect you from something he knows you're either not ready for or something that could potentially ruin your life. Saying no to your children when needed is not being negative, but rather teaching them that they won't get everything in life. You are actually saving them from certain disappointments and from not expecting everything to go their way. You are teaching them to not be entitled but to be more grateful and appreciative. You're teaching them how to deal with rejection in life, because, sadly, we live in a world that chooses who deserves rejection and who deserves acceptance.

Teach them resilience, determination, persistence. Teach them to believe in themselves by how much they value their morals and virtues. We've been taught to believe in words so much that we disregard people's actions as long as they know the right things to say. We focus on listening to only what we want to hear, things that validate our thoughts and beliefs, ideas that are pleasing to our ears, things that boost our egos and make us feel high and mighty, righteous and faultless. Teach your children to pay more attention to what people do than to what they say. Act in ways that teach them what it means to be kind, caring, loving, empathetic, generous, patient, compassionate, and sincere. Don't just tell them, *show* them, because they are watching how you treat others. They are watching how you treat those who are financially less fortunate. Teach your children that their physical attraction doesn't make them beautiful, because at any moment they can lose it. What they own doesn't make them rich, because at any moment it can be gone. But how they care for others, how they take care of those in need, how they help, heal, and make positive changes in the lives of those around them, is what really matters. Teach them that their actions speak louder than their words.

Equally Human. Unequally Unique

Imagine living in a world where we all saw each other as human beings. Not as men or women, not Black or white, not rich or poor, not short or tall, but simply humans. A world filled with love and kindness. Where we teach future generations to be more accepting of each other and less hateful. To create and live healthier lives. To be less greedy, to see each other as more than just someone who can potentially benefit our own self-interests. To be respectful and kind towards one another—not because respecting you or being kind to you will open doors of opportunity, but simply because it's the kind thing to do.

If we all make the conscious decision to heal our wounds and become healthier versions of ourselves, and commit to raising healthy children that are well rounded emotionally, mentally, physically, and psychologically, we can certainly achieve the goal of having a healthier world where children won't need to heal from their parents' traumas and brokenness. When we get to a place where we can teach our boys and girls to see less of their differences and more of their similarities, we'll reach a place of peace, harmony, and inclusivity.

We'll create a society that teaches boys and girls to focus more on their values than their need for acceptance and approval.

But to reach the point of seeing ourselves as equally human, we must teach all children healthy values and ethics. My greatest fear as a father is that the values I'm teaching my daughter are not the values that society will be teaching her. It's no secret that boys and girls are held to different standards. They are taught differently and therefore they process life and relationships differently. Girls are taught at a very young age, whether in their television shows or by societal principles, that someday they'll meet their Prince Charming, get married, and have a family. Boys are taught to become financially driven and not settle down until they find the right girl. But who are these Prince Charmings supposed to be? And who will be the right girls?

Yes, we are all equal because we are all human beings. But we all have our parts to play in each other's lives. If we are not being taught what those parts are, how are we to learn how to play them? You can't raise your sons to be disrespectful to girls and then expect them to respect women when they become men. If they never see a man treating a woman with respect, they won't know how to do it—period. And you can't raise your sons, who have never seen what an emotionally, physically, and spiritually healthy woman acts like, to know how to choose an emotionally healthy woman. So model that, be that, teach them that. Be the woman they are going to marry when the time comes. As fathers, be the man your sons are going to be when they find that emotionally healthy woman to build a family with.

You can't raise daughters without teaching them accountability and expect them to uphold their values and sense of worthiness. You can't expect them to have a healthy relationship when they've never witnessed a healthy relationship. You cannot expect your daughters to respect themselves or a potential partner if their mothers didn't respect themselves or their spouse. You can't expect your daughters to find that emotionally healthy Prince Charming if their father is psychologically unhealthy. But it's not too late to find healing and do right by them. It's not too late to be that wife, that husband, that girlfriend, that partner, that co-parent who teaches them values and morals. Teach them to embrace their uniqueness and that they don't have to be like everyone else or be accepted by everyone in order to be equally human. They are learning to be you by observing what you do and who you are; you are their role models, so teach them by showing them how to be by being the healthiest version of you.

Boys versus Girls

I am troubled by the way society teaches boys and girls to be men and women. In recent years, we have been teaching young girls to be independent, strong, and fierce, while encouraging boys to be soft and less masculine and to embrace their feelings. These are not necessarily negative characteristics, but my concern is that they are not being taught in ways that will facilitate interactions with each other, let alone have healthy future relationships. I feel the need to teach my daughter these things to prepare her to stand her ground, to not depend on others, and to take care of herself; but what we are not teaching them is how to live with each other in a world that pits boys and girls against each other.

We can all agree that boys have been taught the wrong way for a really long time, which has caused a lot of pain to women and to themselves. Boys have been taught to see themselves as the patriarch, independent, rulers, strong, the head, kings, and gods—but this has not worked. Women have had to endure abuse from men who have not been taught kindness, respect, responsibility, and healthy self-worth. Whenever you have people who take greater pride in themselves instead of being kind, generous, loving, respectful, caring, and decent human beings, their self-worth comes into question. When you feel the need to belittle others in order to build your own ego, you are actually insecure, weak, and afraid.

You are holding on to preconceived power that you are afraid can be taken away from you if you stop being callous. Consequently, none of those methods of teaching has helped society or created peaceful and healthy relationships. So when I think of how painful holding such a mindset can be, I refuse to teach my daughter what has caused such agony and dysfunctions in relationships between men and women.

That same toxic mindset has caused our daughters pain by behaving and thinking like the boys. Teaching girls to be independent and strong is dangerous and misleading. We are teaching them to psychologically go against their innate desires, their femininity, and what makes them whole. I've committed to teaching my daughter to be kind and resilient instead of using strength to get through life; to be loving, self-sufficient, and peaceful instead of being aggressive and independent. To be respectful and responsible for herself and to uphold her values. To be understanding and caring, while protecting her self-worth and setting up boundaries. I have committed to teaching her love, and to appreciate and value her gift. Being strong can be lonely. Being independent can be empty, and being aggressive can be detrimental to your health. Teaching girls to fight and stand their ground will give them reasons to always be defensive emotionally, which is a tough way to live.

Punishment and Encouragement

We all need to have a conversation about how we raise, discipline, and communicate with our children. Parents, especially of African descent, have certain ideas about how to discipline children when they do wrong. We're quick to acknowledge their mistakes and shortcomings, but slow to reward and encourage their positive behavior. Would you ever ask your kids if there are things that you could do that would make you a better parent? The answer might be a defensive no, and the logic might be that children don't know what they want and that they should listen and do what their parents say and ask of them.

As a parent, I can imagine where these fears may be coming from. When you give your children an opportunity to be open and honest, they will most likely suggest better and more understanding ways to correct their misbehavior and teach you how to be a healthier parent and a healthier human being. But if you are afraid to face your fear and see your reflection in their eyes, or if you are afraid to face their honest truth about the way you parent, you won't feel comfortable opening that line of conversation.

As parents, we are not perfect. No one teaches us how to be parents; we're all doing the best we know how. So, if we don't see parenting as a partnership between parents and the children, we are psychologically failing our children. We are hurting our kids when we think we own them, instead of understanding that they are a gift to their purpose. We have an opportunity to raise someone who will help and heal their community and their loved ones. Having an open line of communication and valuing their opinions will build trust and healthier relationships with us. We are hurting them when we're quicker to punish them for their inadequacies than encouraging them when they do good. Don't get me wrong. I'm not saying to only see the good they do, because they're human beings and will fall short and will need your guidance and clarity. But remember, you more clearly see the things you look at through magnifying lenses. The plants you water and care for the most will be the ones to blossom more beautifully. So cherish their positive behavior, speak life into the good things they do when they do them. Encourage them by rewarding them when they do the right things; because when they do the wrong things, you won't hesitate to punish them. The more we focus on their misbehavior, the more we encourage negative behavior. We are teaching them to expect the worst in others and subsequently act negatively in order to protect themselves.

Part of our responsibility as parents is to lead our children into adulthood and guide them through paths that will hopefully lead them to a life of purpose. As part of that process, we will have to correct some of their behavior and choices at times. But for most parents who are still broken and wounded, disciplining your children shouldn't mean abuse. It should involve correcting and teaching them in ways that are positive and encouraging, so they have a more positive attitude about doing the right thing. It's an opportunity to pause, change direction, teach, or perhaps connect with them in a vulnerable and not so glorifying moment. Cursing and screaming at your children won't help them; it will hurt them emotionally and spiritually. Showing aggression and anger towards them, when they don't get it right, has everything to do with your mental stability, not necessarily their actions.

Conversely, some parents feel the need to reward their children by providing whatever those children want in order to maintain their love and affection. But rewarding doesn't mean spoiling; it doesn't mean crippling and it doesn't mean making unhealthy sacrifices. It means acknowledging and appreciating good behavior. Don't destroy your children's morale by giving them everything they want and expect.

Growing up in Haiti, where the slavery mentality was still embedded in the culture, adults didn't explain anything to children; no means no, and no questions asked. But understand that it is the master's way; it's not the healthy way. You wouldn't want someone yelling at you and being aggressive with you on a regular basis; it's not healthy for your children, and it's not healthy for you as parents, either. Living in constant emotional turmoil will take a toll on your mental well-being. Teaching your children humility, and how to appreciate sacrifices that you or others make for them, will lessen some of their emotional struggles as adults. Creating healthy memories that they will treasure for the rest of their lives is much more important than the materialistic goods you try to buy their affections with.

I remember listening to this country singer telling a story about how his father taught him how to drive an old truck, and, later on, how he taught his daughters to drive with the memories of his father, hoping that one day his daughters would teach *their* children in memory of him. At the end of the day, that's really all we have. Those loving memories, the ones we can pass down to future generations. They may not notice the sacrifices you make to give them a stable living environment until they're adults, but they'll remember moments they spent with you. Spend time with them, acknowledge their efforts to please you and to do the right thing. Teach and guide them; never degrade and belittle them out of fear and anger.

PROFESS AND FORGIVE

WHEN I USED TO HEAR people say forgiveness is for you, I would cringe and wonder how this made sense. If I'd forgiven someone for whatever wrong they'd done, then I couldn't hold them in contempt anymore. I'd have no more reason to be mad at them and make them pay for whatever hurt they caused me. I wanted to remember, I wanted to be reminded of that hurt because it fueled my anger towards them; it motivated me in some twisted way to hold on to that hurt and the pain. It's like the Haitian proverb says, "Bay kou blye, pote mak sonje" (The one who strikes the blow might easily forget, but the one who wears the scars remembers). But then I realized, while I was being mad at them and constantly reliving that pain and anguish, those folks were living their best lives, going about their business, laughing as if they'd never done anything wrong. And so, forgiving others for their wrongs began to make sense to me. But not like you would think.

My understanding of forgiveness at that point was to erase those folks from my mind, my heart, and my life. Their existence was no longer even a wink in my imagination; they were dead to me. But that wasn't healthy either, because I wasn't really forgiving them. I was still carrying the pain that would push me to seek revenge by allowing their action to dehumanize me and cause me to be unkind even to folks who had nothing to do with my pain. It was my way of coping with that hurt. I was running away from the pain and the people who hurt me.

Then, one day, it started to really make sense to me—this idea of professing, acknowledging, and forgiving myself and others for hurt that I may have caused and hurt that may have been caused towards me. I started to understand that, as human beings, we're all messed up; most of us are still broken and unhealed. And at some point in our lives, we will all hurt others and we will all get hurt by others; but the most important thing is how we choose to respond to those hurts.

Do we allow those hurtful moments to turn into something much bigger than what they were intended to be? A hurt, a crucifixion, a lesson, an indication of where you or others stand emotionally and spiritually, and whether those people are worth sharing your gifts or not? And so, I've professed and acknowledged pain that I have caused intentionally and unintentionally. I've learned to heal and forgive myself for those I may have wronged, and I forgave those who may have wronged me by sympathizing with their brokenness and their hurt—not for their sake, but for mine; forgiveness is for me.

Not holding onto pain that has been inflicted upon me means I am free from the grueling burden of anger, resentment, and revenge; I am free from them and my own detrimental mindset. I've learned to release people and let them go; I've learned to take my gifts away from them and stop sharing. In spite of bearing the scars of someone else's blow, forgiving them releases you from the weight of holding them hostage in your heart and mind. It doesn't mean forgetting their hurtful actions and it doesn't mean giving them another chance or access to your gifts. It means releasing yourself from that person's draining emotional grip, freeing the space they were holding in your heart and mind, and allowing positive and healthier memories to set in.

It's been said that no one gets out of this life alive. I also believe that no one resides in this world unscathed. Our hurt may be different from one another's, but, in order to heal and become our emotionally healthier selves, we all have some professing and forgiving to do. We all need to profess the hurt we've caused others and the hurt others have caused us, and forgive them and ourselves. We all may have someone we need to forgive and we all may have something we need to heal from. That someone may even be yourself, for hurt you've caused to yourself and others, for brokenness you've accepted from others, for failing and quitting, or for never even trying. It may be something you've done for which you are still carrying the burden of guilt and shame.

Voices

One of the best parts of writing this book was having the privilege to hear and read stories from folks who have gone through generational pain in their childhood and adult life: people who have yet to heal from traumatic and detrimental patterns that have left them emotionally shattered and empty. As I reveal the source of my trauma, I extend grace and forgiveness to myself and to those who have caused me pain. I hope my message, along with the stories below, resonate with you and that you too can prayerfully embark on your everlasting healing journey and start living in God's intended purpose for your life.

Dear Broken Daughter,

Sometimes, the world may not be what it was intended to be for you. It may be unkind, unfair, unreceptive, and even cruel. The expectations that have been placed upon you can be quite heavy for such small shoulders to bear. But you've given it your best, you've handled it all with grace and elegance, you've made the best of the worst that has been dealt to you. And even when some of the burdens may seem to be rootless and unsubstantiated, you effortlessly strive for better, healthier, and greater purpose; you ought to be proud. I want you to know that you are unique and unambiguously made. You are beautiful. You are smart. And you are purposefully created. Continue to pick up as many pieces as you can, one at a time, until you complete your puzzle and become emotionally and spiritually whole. You don't need to grow up to be strong; let healing guide you. Courage is within you; let your resilience and purpose motivate you. Vulnerability and humility are for you; embrace them. Gentleness is for your emotional stability; let it blossom. Being strong can be a burden when you feel like you have to carry it to defend yourself, instead of channeling it for the moments that require it; choose wisdom. You are God's most precious creation; thrive on it. Choose to accept and understand others while setting up boundaries to protect your peace and your purpose. You are God's gift to you and to those with untainted eyes who are able to see you as such. Choose to see past the pain and the hurt that has been laid upon you by a strong and fed-up parent as well as society. You have choices, so choose forgiveness, empathy, and understanding; choose healing.

You have a purpose that's greater than life itself; find it and live it. Create healthy legacies and change the world; build lasting memories and live a fulfilled life; inspire current and future generations with your words and actions; help those who aren't able to help themselves and heal those who are broken, lost and hopeless. Your life is meaningful beyond the scope of your own understanding. You. Are. Perfectly. Created.

Sherri shared:

I am a strong woman who has recovered from being a broken daughter. Growing up, I was chubby and teased, which left me emotionally scarred. I wanted to feel loved and accepted, but I was constantly made fun of for what I looked like, instead of who I was. I was a daddy's girl, so when he left before I became a teenager, a sense of who I was and how I was to be loved left with him. But I learned to work hard and take pride in everything I do. The lack of my parents' teaching impacted my life deeply. I learned what not to do in situations just by watching them. I had a lot of self-esteem issues because of my weight, and I learned early on over and over that people are cruel and vicious. My heart has been broken many times from a very young age, and my upbringing showed me how NOT to be.

In spite of having to raise two children on her own, my mother did her best to teach me to work hard, treat people right, and to love God. So she had to be strong even when she felt weak, hurt, and sometimes defeated. My brothers and I tried to keep her sane by being a little crazy so she could laugh and have fun. And as rewarding as those moments may have been, they taught me everything I didn't want to become as a woman.

As an adult, in order to heal and let go of all the pain I had accumulated from my broken childhood, I had to tell my mother about some of the things that had happened between us, or had been said that had hurt me—things she felt I should have done, or how I should have acted or felt. She didn't know she had inflicted a lifetime of hurt on me. But we're cool now. Apologies, hugs, kisses, growth; they were needed. I also was able to tell my dad a few things, too. Dialogue has allowed me to get some things off my chest, and as a woman who still acquires strength to get through life, I now understand in order to live a purposeful and emotionally healthy life, I need to forgive and relinquish my strength and heal from my past traumas.

What I would share with any young girls who have gone through or are still going through those challenges, whether it's self-esteem matters, lack of love from your parents, or feeling broken and empty, is allow God to come into your heart and he will guide your path. We don't get to pick our parents. We don't know what they have been through to get them in the frame of mind that causes them to do what they do or don't do, to say what they say or don't say. Love yourself, love others, be purposeful, be courteous and helpful. We are all here to serve in one capacity or another. Focus on your health and your dreams, and dance as if no one is watching.

You are beautifully made!

You Are More Than Your Current Path

Your pathway to healing may require you to give up the life you now have and start over. None of us were created to live a depressed and unfulfilled life, but, somehow, we've settled for it in one form or another. For some of us, our paths may have been chosen for us by our parents and the circumstances we were born into; for others, our brokenness may have driven us into making choices that have depleted us, robbed us of our purpose, left us hopeless and empty. We have devoted ourselves as sacrificial favors to broken relationships, disparaging friendships, and mean-spirited behavior that destroys, demonizes, and dehumanizes us. But I believe through healing, we can all reach a deeper level of acceptance, understanding, and empathy, and an untiring desire to serve our purpose by helping and healing one another.

Dear Strong Woman,

If you knew how life would have turned out, I'm not sure you would have done anything differently. You have been created with the gift of unparalleled and compassionate love. In spite of all the pain you've endured, all the trauma life may have thrown in your direction, you still manage to find it within you to smile, to thrive, and to love again; and for that, you are God's pure gift to the universe. From your magical womb that blossoms the seeds of our fathers, you are the purest form of earth; you are mesmerizing. Your womanly virtues, your courage, dedication, compassion, and forte are borne of vulnerability, humility, and grace. Your mind and spirit create havens of comfort for your sons and daughters, for you are divinely made in the image of the Creator. You are incomparable. You are an earthly goddess. May healing be yours. May you find truth in your burden and restoration in your quest to become whole again. May you find everlasting and purposeful self-love; may grace be extended to you, and may peace become your ornament. You are loved; embrace that feeling. You are whole; recognize that truth. You are extraordinary; honor that virtue. And most of all, you are purposefully and stunningly made; live and illuminate that life.

Jenny shared:

To my fellow broken women and daughters, I say: you didn't get to this place in life by yourself and you won't heal by yourself either. Reflecting back on life thus far, I can identify as a broken daughter who has had to become a strong woman due to circumstances. I grew up with both of my parents in a household that seemed pretty normal to me as a child, but, looking back now, I realize it was not healthy.

My mother worked, she cooked, she cleaned, and she was always pleasant. My father worked, he fixed things around the house (or he at least tried), and he told the family what they were and weren't going to do. Growing up, I was taught a woman should be all of these things and do all of these things, even though it might never be enough. During my young adult life, I often thought I would not be like my mom and end up with nothing. I found myself frequently fighting these roles because I did not want to end up like my mother, in her early-60s, divorced and alone. From there, I was a broken daughter and learned to be a strong mother.

As a broken daughter, I have carried dysfunctional habits from my childhood and adolescence into my adult life, which has hindered my ability to trust people, be vulnerable, and, to some extent, show empathy. Maintaining optimism during relationships has been difficult. I recently deduced that I am, and have been, someone who is often committed in a noncommittal kind of way. I enjoy and yearn for relationships most people steer clear of, such as long-distance relationships, because I can be as committed (and comfortable with) as I want, without having to fully commit myself to having this person around in my space too often. By keeping this distance, in my mind it lessens the chance of this person getting too close and, in turn, the chance of me becoming vulnerable and eventually ending up getting hurt.

Having to be a strong woman has not made it easy to be in a relationship either. Having that "I got it" mentality oftentimes pushes people away. When I had my son, someone told me to be sure not to take on the role of his dad because I needed to allow space for his father to be a dad; but when I saw him coming up short, I often stepped in and got things done. I have now realized that was the best advice I have ever been given. I allowed my mind and circumstances to make me think I needed to be strong when, in reality, my life and/or circumstances were not calling for that at all. Being a strong woman has been embedded into my psyche, and this has not been ideal for my romantic relationships. Men are supposed to fill certain roles and being a "strong woman" robs them of these experiences and opportunities, eventually emasculating them, and no man wants to feel less than a man, ever.

Growing up as a daddy's girl, I was spoiled and loved by my father, but even then, I always knew in no way, would I ever wish a man like my father on anyone, let alone myself. I can honestly say my father stepped up and became a father at a very young age; he did what he thought was the right thing to do, but in the midst of that, he hurt many people. Even as adults, I still subject to deep hurts by my father. My father is certainly not the type of man I seek as a partner, husband, or father to my children, but I worry that the way I commit, without committing, I am more like him than I ever realized.

My mother and I are absolute opposites, and I intentionally made sure of this. Growing up, I watched my mother work extremely hard, but that did not stop the abuse she received from my dad. Somewhere in my mind I began to think the reason she was mistreated was because she was docile and weak; and, of course, I learned to become the opposite of that. I approach my personal and romantic life with a certain level of assertiveness, which comes off as aggressive and unbearable at times. I have only recently learned that these traits are defense mechanisms I have built in order to make sure I do not endure what she's had to endure; but really deep down under these traits, I am realizing I am more like my mother than I thought. By portraying an aggressive and strong persona, I've gotten in situations and relationships that were the opposite of what I've hoped for.

Although I have always been someone who reflected on past experiences and life, it was not until recently that I realized I needed to process the things from my past that still have a stranglehold on my life. I am hoping I find the right therapist for me and my son because I have passed on some unintended trauma and characteristics to him, and I should make sure he knows help is always available to him and to reject the stigma of psychological healing in our communities.

If I could give any advice to broken daughters, I would tell them not to internalize the unhealthy patterns they learned growing up, because detrimental behavior does not have to be a part of the life they choose. As a mother I will continuously remind my son that his mom is doing what she thinks is the best and right for him, even if it doesn't always look and feel that way. My advice to strong women would be to stop being so strong; you don't have to be; your children and those who care for you will be better for it. Continue your search for wellness and healing and one day you will live an intentionally fulfilling and purposeful life.

Defining Yourself

Protectors, providers, hunters, and conquerors. All of us boys were born with these innate traits, but somehow, we've been taught to reject them. We have been trained to despise the very traits that we were created to uphold and utilize to serve our purpose. Somewhere along the way, those characteristics misled us into succumbing to our greed, ignorance, and a false sense of power. They led us to believe in our false superiority, which hurts, breaks, brutalizes, and dehumanizes others. And with that teaching, we have rejected our purpose to help and to heal one another. We ought to profess and forgive ourselves and each other for our destructive ways, while seeking healthier and more selfless ways to turn back to living a life that is emotionally, spiritually, and physically healed and purposefully driven.

Dear Defeated Son,

If I could get inside your mind and help you understand your influence, your potential, I'd leap through lethal spears and jagged flames just to make you realize that you are powerful. Descendent of Africa, you are royal. Bred from the motherland, groomed by dark fiery soils and sunsets, you are mystical. Misunderstood, feared, abandoned, yet risen, you are pioneering. It's not easy being you sometimes, but still you shine bright even when darkness creeps and shadows darken your light; still you prosper. Revolutionize cultures and break down barriers, innovate new paths to rise; you are a gift.

The cards have not been stacked fairly, it seems, but you've gracefully handled the cards you were dealt, Lord knows. Generational psychological stigmas have shamed you, dragged you, and held you down. It's time. Time to rise against self-oppression and healing barriers. The time is now; claim it. You deserve healing. Healing from what should have been done but never was. Healing from those who should have been there for you but never were; you matter. Your life matters. Your peace of mind matters. Your achievements matter. Your purpose matters. Even though the roads may seem uneven and the odds may pile up, healing and forgiveness are self-driven roads to your purpose; seek them. The roots may seem shallow and the grounds may be unsteady; plant your seeds. Seeds of forgiveness, grace, and healing. Grab your brothers' hands; they need you. Manhood will come; don't rush it, learn it. Your purpose is greater than your circle, but start there, elevate one another. Create havens even in the midst of the struggles; it's needed. And although the clouds may seem to last longer than the sunshine, be brave, be consistent, be kind, be bold, be healed, be understanding, be empathetic, and, most of all, be purposeful; it's in you.

Ben shared:

I never thought one day I'd be willingly talking about my feelings, let alone revealing my weaknesses to anyone, but today I am. Growing up in the eighties in a gang- and violence-infested neighborhood, the only way out at times felt like it was kill or be killed. My mother worked two jobs so we could have a place to live, so I pretty much raised myself and my younger sister. I have a vague memory of my dad; the moments we spent together were barely moments, because I would only see him in the neighborhood, running the streets with his gang friends before he got arrested. He is now serving life in prison.

My sister never met him. Watching friends and cousins selling drugs to make money so they can help at home, deep down inside I knew that wasn't the life I wanted for myself and my sister. I remember working at a barbershop for a few hours after school, sweeping the floors and cleaning up, so I could have some money and help my mom a bit. There were times when I felt like giving up trying to be different and join a gang too. Even though I had cousins who would protect me so I wouldn't get mugged, I felt like I needed to be my own man, carry my own weight, protect myself; but I knew my mom would kill me. I knew she wanted what was best for us, but I don't think she understood my struggles, though. Watching your friends and family getting killed, your father in prison, it felt like my destiny was chosen for me.

I remember when my mom got sick and she couldn't go to work; I was fourteen or so and we didn't have any money for food or to pay the rent. We got kicked out and we went to live with my grandmother. The part that breaks you down is not really the struggles, but feeling like there's no escaping this life, this system. Your parents were born into it, their parents were born into it, at some point you just feel defeated and start wondering what makes me different, why would I be the one to get away from this?

I wish my dad were around sometimes. Even though my mom did her best to give my sister and me everything she could, my heart broke watching her dying daily, working so hard and raising us on her own.

If only she could have seen us right now. Both my sister and I have great careers and living a life we could have only dreamed of back then. My mom got shot one night coming home from work by some guys who thought she was somebody else; it hurts and I miss her, a lot.

As a boy, the streets taught me how to be a man. I had to grow up fast because I had responsibilities to take care of; I had to help my mom and my sister and myself too. Being an adult now, I still struggle with a lot of things I was never taught by a father figure. I've figured out a lot of things on my own and they haven't always been the right things, but I'm trying. With three kids of my own now, I know what kind of father I don't want to be, but not necessarily the kind to be, because I never witnessed it. But what I know for certain is that I would never abandon my kids because that hurts and you feel unwanted, unloved, even as an adult. So I'm giving being a father to my children my absolute best, at least as best as I've learned how over the years.

I've learned to forgive my dad because he didn't know better. My mom did her best and I loved and appreciated her for her sacrifices. But had we not moved to my grandmother's house, I would have probably ended up like my dad; who knows? A lot of my friends and cousins ended up like their dads, in prison or dead. Those streets have a way of knocking you down, especially when you're already down. But back then I knew I had a much bigger purpose than the streets and the violence I grew up around; now I'm doing everything possible to help young boys who are in the position I was in to see the bigger picture, the life outside of the 'hood. I'm still healing from some of my traumas and I have a long way to go. But my purpose is to help others find their way and become who they were meant to be. I'm still struggling with having a healthy romantic relationship because I never saw it growing up, but I'm confident with consistent efforts, healing, and lots of letting go and awareness, I'll get there.

To young boys who are feeling defeated, hopeless, abandoned and misguided, I'm begging you—learn forgiveness. Learn to forgive yourself, your parents, and anyone who hurt you. Learn empathy and healing because the more you can understand and empathize with your past and the things that hurt you, the sooner you can let them go and heal from them. I was angry and that anger only hurt me, so try to understand that your mom and your dad did, or are doing, the best with what they have—emotionally, spiritually, and financially. Appreciate them while you have them, if you have them. Cherish good memories and use the ones that have broken you down as stepping-stones to do better and become healthier. Heal from your pain, believe in yourself, do the smart thing, learn healthier habits, be purposeful, and God will make a way.

Breaking with Your Past

Understanding your past and your history can help you create a new narrative for yourself and your future, because only then will the past help you understand the present and restructure the future. Sometimes we get stuck in a generational merry-go-round and we never get to understand the foundation of those patterns. We try to make surface changes only to find ourselves right back where we started. As African-descent men, the root of our dysfunction comes from a lack of understanding of our foundation. Whether we choose to go back to pre-slavery or post-slavery, until we learn who we were and where we came from, who we are will be a reflection of who we don't intend to be. Like the saying goes: you can't outrun your past. But the worst part about an unknown past is not knowing which past you're facing in the present. Although you can't change the past, understanding who you were and where you came from will make you realize that you are an empire, lineage of kings and lions; it's time to claim your throne, it's time to rise and live purposefully.

Dear Fed-Up Man,

You are influential beyond comprehension. Born of spears and arrows, from the ashes of your African roots to the royalty of your ancestors, you are a reflection of God. You are the representation of kings and heroes, lovers and creators. You were made for greatness. Innovative, compassionate, physically and emotionally empowered, you are a warrior, descendent of healers and hunters; you are a protector. Claim your throne. Elevate your purpose, sway it like a flag of honor, take your place, kneel at the healing circle, clutch your triumph, raise your peace of mind; that is your calling. Conquer your defeats, and let your purpose praise you. Find your courage in the valleys and under the deep oceans; let not these sacrifices go in vain; revive them with scorching flames. Raise your hand and grip your fists; healing is yours, and you don't need to be good when you are actually NOT good.

Kindness is courage, love is wisdom, respect is humility, understanding is empathy; take some, share some; it's yours, reach out and lend some, open those healing doors. Emotional and spiritual freedom is free; take some, share some. Our sons and daughters bleed tears, as you fight back your fears. Face them and own them, you got this, healing is supreme. Flee not, my brother, the victory is only a battle when you hang on to unhealed sorrows that defeat your tomorrows. So let go, break free, take hold of pure and healthy intentions that allow your restoration to ignite your purpose and breathe life into your kings and queens. You are intentionally created!

Christian shared:

My understanding of being a man, I realized early on, was embedded in the twisted idea that I was superior. Watching my father dictate everything that went on in the house, I learned that was what men do; they take charge and everyone else follows. But becoming an adult, being in the real world, I realized that wasn't the way life works, because that superiority complex is not a recipe for team playing or a healthy relationship. My father was a godly man and, therefore, every aspect of our being had a biblical affiliation to it. I have taken pride in being a man and do what I was taught men are supposed to do: work hard, provide, show little to no emotion because that's weakness, and be there for your loved ones. I was brought up to be respectful of others, kind, and honest; but those qualities held little value growing up in a culture and a community that embraced fast money, flashy things, and popularity.

To the outside world, our lives seemed perfect; but, at home, the verbal and the emotional abuse were frightening. I'm in my early fifties now and I can still hear my parents yelling at each other and slamming doors when they'd think I was asleep. It's sad to say, even though I admire and respect both of my parents for their sacrifices and for loving me as much as they knew how amidst their own struggles, I knew when I grew up I never wanted to be like my dad, nor did I want to marry a woman like my mom. I had a traditional family dynamic, where both of my parents were, and are, still together—miserably. When it comes to healthy relational patterns, I can't even use my parents as role models because of their damaging, unhealthy habits; they mainly taught me dysfunctions. I grew up hurting and resenting my father for the man he was and the way he treated my mom; and I rejected the woman my mother was for constantly lashing out at my dad and arguing with him. So I ended up learning to be someone different out of my hurt and pain, which created someone even more hurt and broken.

I got married in my late thirties and had in my mind everything I didn't want in a marriage, everything I didn't want to become, and everything I didn't want in a partner; but I had no idea what I wanted, so I ended up having everything I didn't want. I've now been divorced for almost three years and I never even really understood what went wrong. After almost ten years of marriage, we became everything my parents were in their marriage and everything my ex-wife's mother was, raising her without her father; we became them and it was unhealthy and exhausting, not just for us, but more so for our kids.

Now as a parent, I have been dedicating my energy to healing from everything I didn't know was driving me and dictating some of my hurtful behavior. Growing up with resentment and anger for the people who are supposed to be the ones you look up to, I realize, had destroyed me emotionally and spiritually. The kind of man I said I would have never become, I became. I tried so hard to run away from my father's ways; but that's who I was taught to be. It helped me stay out of trouble with the law, it taught me a lot of great principles and work ethics, but emotionally I was immature and not prepared for a healthy and fulfilling relationship with the opposite sex.

As difficult as it may be, as parents we need to understand the level of emotional destruction we can cause our children when we ourselves are emotionally unhealthy. I know it's not easy to admit that you could be hurting your kids when all you want to do for them is what's best; but the honest truth is, if you are not healthy for you, whether emotionally, spiritually or physically, chances are you can't be healthy enough to give and teach them how to be healthy. Personally, I thought I was being great and doing my best, until I started to face some of my own struggles and realized how my children and my loved ones were getting the short end of my version of best. I was great with strangers, because I could be who I wanted to be with them for a limited amount of time. But when I was in my comfort zone and around people who loved me and I could take for granted, I was who I was taught to be—and that wasn't always healthy.

All of us are born with the innate ability to love, to protect, to sacrifice for, and to care for our loved ones, and a lot of us are amazing at doing so. But for those of us who have yet to face our unhealthy childhood patterns, those of us who are still hurting and driven by our pain and everything we don't want, based on our past hurt, I urge you to seek healing because they don't ever really go away on their own. You can bury them, neglect them, get used to them, and even make excuses for them by blaming everyone else, but until you heal, it will be extremely hard to have and maintain healthy relationships with friends, a partner, and even your own children. You will never be at peace with yourself and you may find yourself constantly chasing happiness like I was, instead of finding peace within yourself.

My advice to men who have been defeated and fed up with their lives, is to heal from your brokenness and understand that healing is important, it's needed, it's for you, and it is attainable. During your journey, there will be people in your life who may not understand your process; I've been there. It's okay to distance yourself from anyone who is comfortable in their dysfunction while making you feel guilty for seeking help for your emotional and mental well-being. This journey is for you and anyone willing to take it with you.

Finding Restoration

The road to healing and living purposefully will not be a straight line. There will be bumps along the way as you face heartbreaks, and rivers to cross as you shed tears, mountains to climb as you lie awake in your sleepless nights, and barriers to breakdown as you become misunderstood and alone. But it's a rewarding journey, and it can only be embarked on by you. For some, it may be in the form of forgiveness and letting go of detrimental relationships and friendships; for others, it may be learning to set boundaries in order to maintain your peace of mind and your mental stability. It may be extending forgiveness and moving on, without receiving that apology from someone who may have wronged you. It may be taking some time away from your destructive and depleting environment to psychologically restore, replenish, and restock.

It doesn't mean that you won't be tempted and that those detrimental patterns and burdens won't try to creep back into your life; but when it happens, when they do try, when that insecurity mindset tries to creep in, when that anxiety attack tries to overtake your present joy, remember why you started the journey in the first place, and try to resist falling back into those same patterns by taking necessary healing steps. So whatever it may be for you, however long it may take you, however painful it may get, remember this is for you, and only you can either choose to improve you or allow you to mentally and psychologically deteriorate; and only you can choose rebirth or to stay buried in your crucifixions.

Here are a few steps to consider on your healing journey:

Get Out of Your Comfort Zone

For many of us, the idea of change can be frightening. You may have been living in your dysfunctional patterns for so long, a new way of life may not even seem practical. But in order to seek and find healing, it will require a conscious and intentional decision to get out of your comfort zone and take healthy and constructive risks. You will need to relinquish negative notions, whether it is fear of being judged for trying or not knowing what change will feel like. You will need to conquer those fears and leave your comfort zone and become brave enough to take the first step. You may even resort to skepticism because you've never taken time to do anything significant for yourself, and the idea of giving back to you is foreign. But I want you to know and believe that you are worth every single bit of your self-care, self-love, self-healing, and self-fulfillment. Own it, because no one deserves it more than you do. You are worth it.

Acknowledgment

When you can acknowledge that you have some healing to do, you will most likely be motivated to start taking steps towards facing your traumas or whatever it is you may need to heal from. But if you are not in a place where you can recognize that your detrimental habits are damaging to yourself and others, change will never take place. It's not always easy to identify your own flaws and shortcomings, even if you are an insightful and self-reflective person; you may miss some of your own blind spots, and there's nothing wrong with that as long as you're willing to learn and grow. I remember when my business partner Jackie and I started our Fit For Life Program, a six-week fitness journey to get people in their forties and up to reclaim their health and wellness and become the healthiest version of themselves. One thing she did as a therapist was ask everyone to complete an exercise where they'd ask five to six people they trusted to give them some honest feedback (positive or negative) about them. They would ask specific open-ended questions with no expectations about the answers. This is tricky and may backfire on you and whomever you ask, especially if you are someone who doesn't handle criticism well, or you are not prepared to hear how others see you. But it's a great way to gain some honest insight about yourself; and from there, you can select whatever is feasible to work on without stripping away the basic principles of your being.

A few checkpoint questions to ask yourself while you are on that journey:

What are my relationships with my loved ones like?

We can all find fault in others and identify their wrongdoing, but being aware of your own actions and wrongdoing is the foundation for your personal growth. Focusing on others and their faults only takes away from your focus on your own healing process. If some people are detrimental to your well-being, you have the right to re-evaluate your relationship with them. The fact is, we can all be healthier and we can all act healthier. So if you truly believe that we were all created with purpose, let's start being in each other's lives with a purpose.

Am I my kindest to my loved ones?

We are our unapologetically true selves when we are around people we are closest to. When we are comfortable, we don't have to think about what we say, how we act, or how we react. But this is a double-edged sword, because, in one fell swoop, that mindset can lead to disrespect, entitlement, selfishness, and ungratefulness. If you are not aware of your behavior when you are with people you love, chances are they may not always get the healthiest version of you. Being aware of your behavior will yield to healthier interactions, not just with strangers but also with the people you love most and whom you wouldn't want to lose.

Do I treat people the way I want to be treated?

We all want to be treated kindly, with respect, understanding, empathy, and love. But do you treat others the way you want to be treated? When you love yourself healthfully, you will be kind and respectful to yourself, and, in turn, you will love and be kind to others because you will understand that they too deserve to be treated with love and kindness. Be aware of the way you treat the people in your life, and determine whether or not you treat them in the way that you want to be treated.

Do I give them what I expect to receive?

At our core, we all know we want and deserve to be treated well, whether we choose to act on that knowledge or not. When it comes to dealing with others, especially those we are closest to, we have a certain level of expectation. We want to be prioritized, we want to feel like we matter most and expect to be treated as such. Often our expectations are a one-way street; we expect to receive more than we give. And what we do give is expected to be given back tenfold. A quick self-reflection will help you determine if you are giving what you are expecting to receive. Learn to share with your loved ones and others what you hope will be shared with you, while setting up boundaries and not overextending and oversharing yourself.

Do I extend grace when it's needed, as I would expect it to be extended to me?

It's not easy extending grace, particularly when you've been hurt and betrayed, but it is essential. Whether you choose to extend it to someone you are no longer with is your choice. As broken individuals, even after we find healing and become mindful of our actions, we will fall short; we make mistakes, we hurt our loved ones, and they hurt us. But in order to receive that grace, you too must be willing and able to extend it when it is needed. Extending grace and forgiveness doesn't mean putting yourself in harm's way or in a situation where you will be taken advantage of. Learn what you can tolerate, learn what's healthy, and extend grace and forgiveness for you and for your peace of mind; allow others to do the same, because they too deserve to have peace of mind.

Am I helping them grow or am I hindering their growth?

Sometimes we unintentionally dissuade others from growing emotionally, spiritually, and even physically. Our intention to do right by them may be pure, but we may be unaware that our behavior can be damaging. You might think you're encouraging someone to become healthier by telling them what they want to hear because you don't want to hurt their feelings; but, in reality, you are enabling a negative behavior or a way of thinking that initially caused them to be where they are. Spiritually, if you have a pessimistic view on life, you are not helping those around you grow, because they may either feel the need to join you where you are or have to constantly go out of their way to lift your spirit up. This can drain them more than you realize. Physically, if someone close to you embarks on a journey to become healthier, and you judge them for it or purposely do things to negate their efforts, you are not helping them. Being aware of how your behavior affects others will help you create healthier and more meaningful relationships with your loved ones and with the world around you.

Do I understand their purpose and do I help fuel it?

If you are not helping the people in your life grow, become mentally, spiritually and physically healthier, and live more purposeful lives, not only are you not living in your purpose, but you are not in their lives for the right purpose. It doesn't mean you will have to carry their weight and continuously hold their hands, but the way you live your life and interact with others should be purposeful and should inspire health and growth. We can all be part of others' lives for self-serving reasons. It may be a way to pass the time; to have someone to gossip with, someone to transfer your pain and bad days onto, someone to fill an empty space; we can be with someone for all those reasons and still do nothing to help fuel their purpose. Not everyone is ready and willing to live a healthier and purposeful life, but your goal and purpose for being in someone else's life should not be to encourage or facilitate their dysfunctional and harmful behavior. Although it is not your job to fix others or carry their burdens, the relationship should be mutually helpful and beneficial, in that your presence should help others heal and live healthier and more purposeful lives.

Finding Help

After you acknowledge that you have some healing to do, and not necessarily what you need to heal from, find someone who can help you understand your struggles and help you to take the necessary steps towards your healing process. I believe in prayers, but as a Christian and someone who has prayed and received steady prayers for my emotional troubles, let me encourage you by saying we need more than prayers—we need human guidance. God created us with the ability and the purpose to help and heal one another. Finding someone who's qualified and able to guide you in your journey is crucial.

Prayers will help, but, as the saying goes, God helps those who help themselves. I also understand we have friends who are there for us whenever we may need them; but you can't rely on your friends who are going through similar troubles simply because you can relate to each other's traumas. They need guidance too, and chances are, as much as they may be able to support and be there for you, they may be sinking you deeper into your emotional abyss. Most of your friends will tell you what you want to hear in order to help you cover your pain. And in the same way many of us don't know how to face our own trauma, many of your friends would prefer not to face someone else's either.

Some questions to consider when seeking a counselor or therapist:

Can they understand my struggles?

Some therapists may be great at what they do, but they may still be unable to understand your struggles. In fact, they may not even know how to help you, and that is okay. Your experiences are yours, you went through them; they affected you and only you know how much. Don't take it personally if others don't understand them; they may not be familiar with what you have gone through. However, you need to find someone who is able to understand them. Search the Internet, and don't be ashamed to ask around for recommendations for someone who will be the perfect helper and healer for you.

Am I comfortable being honest with them, and do we have a connection?

I know it's not a matchmaking process, but finding someone you feel safe and easy being vulnerable with is crucial. If you don't feel comfortable being honest and completely transparent with your counselor, he or she may not be the right one for you. Or maybe you are still in your comfort zone and feel the need to hide your struggles. Self-analyze yourself; remember this is for you and for the betterment of yourself and your healing journey. Counselors don't judge and they won't minimize your troubles, whether it's feeling overwhelmed and not being in control of your life or not knowing how to set boundaries and maintain your peace of mind. Your struggles are yours and only you know how much they affect you.

Are they being honest with me or are they training me to be a long-term patient/client?

Not that you want to rush your process, but keep in mind that some people are in their professions mainly to make a living and that involves recurring businesses. So being mindful of your progress and improvement is important. Make the efforts, go through the changes, and follow the plan being put in place for your healing process.

Do they have a plan for my healing process?

A well-rounded counselor will create a healing plan for your process. They will give you helpful steps to follow and "homework" to do between sessions. If you find yourself repeating the same steps after weeks of therapy and don't see any noticeable progress, you may not be with the right counselor for you. Again, there is no specific time stamp on your healing process and it may take a long time before you see substantial progress, but stick with it while being mindful of your progress. It took a lifetime to get to where you are now, so it will take some time to heal. And healing is what the process is all about.

Responsibility

It may not have been our fault that we have been hurt and living with anger and resentment, but we are responsible to heal from those wounds. Taking responsibility for our behavior, the way we respond or didn't respond to our trauma, is ours and ours alone. We know what we are going through; only we know how those things impacted us and made us feel, so only we can change them, whether it is with the help of a mental health professional or a respected, healed, loved one. The journey is our responsibility and ours alone.

Accountability

Sometimes we are equal participants in our brokenness, which is more than we are willing and able to admit. We all make mistakes, as well as choices we are not proud of; after all, we are fallible and broken beings. Being accountable for our actions and our behavior serves us by helping us avoid repeating similar mistakes or patterns that caused us psychological and even physical harm. Holding ourselves accountable for events that may have caused us hurt doesn't mean we are taking the blame; it's a way to simply reassure ourselves that we understand what transpired and that we won't repeat our past mistakes or the hurt we may have caused others. The inability to hold ourselves culpable for our negative actions towards others will prevent us from being genuinely remorseful and empathetic.

IN CONCLUSION

As I've said, before writing this book I was going through my own healing process. I recall having a conversation with a colleague about my burning vision to help people heal psychologically and finding emotional restoration. As optimistic as I had always known my friend to be, his response was a bit cynical. It wasn't that he didn't believe that it was my calling or that I couldn't do it, but he was skeptical because he believed that we, as African-descent people, were far too self-protective to change and that my brothers and sisters would not be open to the possibility of emotional healing and living in our God's ordained purpose for us. But clearly, I believe otherwise.

This book isn't a step-by-step guide to healing, but rather an examination of the way we live our lives and a plea to become a healthier, greater, and more purposeful version of ourselves. As you have read, I explain how our parents taught and raised us to be who we are and, in some way, to be who *they* are. And in order for us to become who we were meant to be, and break free from our detrimental generational patterns and traditions that keep us broken, hurt, unloved, empty, depressed, angry, and resentful, we must be willing to find healing and create new, healthy patterns that will better serve us. We must heal so we can be healthier role models for our children and future generations.

Many of us have all been through trauma and experiences that have left us wounded and scarred. Some of us have healed, others have put up protective walls in order to avoid getting hurt. Additionally, we also carry our unresolved discontentment, resentments, and disappointments through our lives and end up being more hurt and causing more pain to others. We live on a highly emotional plane, not knowing when we're going to get hurt by others or when we may cause hurt to others.

I hope this book has helped you grasp your true potential and develop a tireless goal for what you were created to accomplish in this life. I pray that you have discovered your calling and that you understand that we are all created with a purpose that's far greater than ourselves. I pray that your healing journey is as rewarding and fulfilling as the destination of living in your purpose. Life can be fulfilling if you allow your principles and actions to guide you to the right path. Love is the basis of our existence; aim for it, find it, live it, and share it.

Through self-care, self-love, understanding, wisdom, professing, and forgiveness, may healing be yours and your loved ones. May the fulfillment of your purpose guide you to a life that is filled with joy, laughter, and endless memories. May your love and connections be purposefully driven. May you live a life that is intentional, kind, empathetic, generous, thoughtful, loving, healthy, fruitful and, most importantly, purposeful. May God bless you, and may God bless your healing process.

SELF-DEVELOPMENT

Living A Purposeful Life

1 Peter 4:10 says, "Each of you should use whatever gift you have received to serve others, as faithful stewards of God's grace in its various forms." God has created us as gifts for our own purpose and for one another. He has blessed each of us with a unique calling to fulfill that purpose. He has numbered our days and granted us the ability to use our gifts to serve others. Our actions, our choices, the way we treat others, and the legacies we leave behind will define whether or not we have lived our purpose and fulfilled God's intention for us.

Our past and present circumstances can keep us from living the life we were called to live. At times we may feel empty, broken, and stuck. We may fall short of our efforts to live a meaningful life. We may get sidetracked by the consequences of our choices and pay the price of pain that has been inflicted upon us.

I hope this book reminds you that it is not over yet. You are blessed with the ability to shatter generational pain, inherited dysfunctions, and to start building the life you were meant to live. Depression doesn't have to be part of the life you want to create. Failure does not have to define your existence. Self-hate, past hurt, and disappointments don't have to deprive you of a life filled with love, grace, and, most of all, peace of mind. Fear doesn't have to own you. Your mistakes don't have to define your present and future. You were created with a purpose far greater than what you have experienced. A purpose to flourish and blossom, and to live a contented and memorable life. A purpose to love, heal, and to help those in need of the gift you have to offer. It is in you and it is with you.

I encourage you to ask yourself if you are living a purposeful life. Examine the way you love, treat yourself, and others. Reflect on your daily interactions. Listen to the words you speak. Are they intentional and mindful? Do your actions propel growth, healing, and oneness? Are you living a purposeful life?

Broken Daughter:

A girl who grew up feeling an emotional, physical, and spiritual void, overwhelmed by a lack of parental connection and love. She has experienced traumatic events and disappointments during her childhood.

Stronger Woman:

A broken daughter who had to endure life's challenges, failed relationships, and disappointments. She grew up using her emotional and spiritual strength to make it through life without healing from her past traumas. She frequently has to muscle through challenging times filled with hurt, resentment, fear, self-reliance, and independency.

Defeated Boy:

A boy who has been overcome by the adversity of his childhood experiences, often feeling inadequate, unimportant, stuck, and estranged. He had to prematurely become a man in order to provide, protect, and care for himself and his family, only to meet with a failure to succeed. A boy who feels lost and empty; who is unwittingly paying for his father's shortfalls.

Fed-Up Man:

A defeated boy who carries his childhood traumas into his adult life and becomes tired and frustrated with himself, his life, and his surroundings. He often feels unappreciated, unheard, and misunderstood. He is tired of living up to the expectations of others.

Questions to Reflect On:

1. Do you consider yourself to be a Broken Daughter and/ or a Strong Woman; or a Defeated Son and/or a Fed-up Man needing to heal from hurtful and disappointing past experiences?

2. How have any of these characteristics helped or hurt you in your daily life? How have they impacted your relationships with your children and with the opposite sex?

3. How have the teachings of your parents affected your childhood and adult life?

4. Daughters: How does your mother reflect the woman you aspire to be? How has your mother influenced you as a woman, wife, and partner? Is your father the type of man you seek as a partner, husband, and father to your children?

5. Sons: How does your father reflect the man you aspire to be? How has your father influenced you as a man, husband, and partner? Is your mother the type of woman you seek as a partner, wife, and mother to your children?

6. How has your upbringing affected your decisions as a child and as an adult?

7. Daughter: How has your mother's pain affected your life and romantic relationships?

8. Son: Do you feel the need to make up for your father's shortcomings?

9. What steps have you taken towards healing and learning who you were meant to be instead of who your parents taught you to be?

10. Parents: What are you doing differently to help raise mentally, spiritually, emotionally, and physically healthier children?

11. What is your purpose and how do you plan to live a purposeful life?

12. What advice would you give to a Broken Daughter, Defeated Son, Strong Woman, and Fed-up Man after reading the book?

The Purposeful Living Challenge

Mark wants to challenge you to take a closer look at your relationships with those closest to you and start evaluating them with an open mind. The goal is to build and create relationships that are fulfilling, healthy, and purposeful.

Are you ready for the challenge?

1. *In a few words, describe your relationships with your loved ones?*

2. *Ask yourself, am I my kindest to my loved ones?*

3. *Do I treat people the way I want to be treated?*

4. *Do I give to others what I expect to receive?*

5. *Do I extend grace when it's needed, as I would expect it to be extended to me?*

6. *Am I helping others grow or am I hindering their growth?*

7. *Do I understand others' purpose and do I help fuel it?*

8. *Based on what you read in the book about purposeful living and purposeful love, can you describe the kind of relationship you want to build with family, friends, and a partner?*

9. *What is the hardest part for you when it comes to your healing process?*

10. *What's the first step you will take towards healing and living a purposeful life?*

ADDITIONAL READINGS

1) https://www.columbiapsychiatry.org/news/addressing-mental-health-black-community

2) Stigma Regarding Mental Illness among People of Color - BH365 (thenationalcouncil.org)

3) Banks, Kira Hudson and Kohn-Wood, Laura P., "Gender, Ethnicity and Depression: Intersectionality in Mental Health Research with African American Women" (2002). Scholarship. Paper 6.

4) http://digitalcommons.iwu.edu/psych_scholarship/6

5) https://digitalcommons.iwu.edu/cgi/viewcontent.cgi?article=1005&context=psych_scholarship

6) https://racereflections.co.uk/wp-content/uploads/2014/05/racism-and-mental-health-the-african-american-experience.pdf

7) Ward, E. C., Clark, l., & Heidrich, S. (2009). African American Women's beliefs, coping behaviors, and barriers to seeking mental health services. Qualitative health research, 19(11), 1589–1601. https://doi.org/10.1177/1049732309350686

8) Wilkins, E.J., Whiting, J.B., Watson, M.F. et al. Residual Effects of Slavery: What Clinicians Need to Know. Contemp Fam Ther 35, 14–28 (2013). https://doi.org/10.1007/s10591-012-9219-1

9) **Cultural Trauma: Slavery and the Formation of African American Identity.** By Ron Eyerman

10) Murry, V.M., Bynum, M.S., Brody, G.H. et al. African American Single Mothers and Children in Context: A Review of Studies on Risk and Resilience. Clin Child

Fam Psychol Rev 4, 133–155 (2001). https://doi.org/10.1023/A:1011381114782

11) Ellen M. Chiocca, American Parents' Attitudes and Beliefs About Corporal Punishment: An Integrative Literature Review, Journal of Pediatric Health Care, 10.1016/j.pedhc.2017.01.002, 31, 3, (372-383), (2017). (https://onlinelibrary.wiley.com/doi/abs/10.1002/j.2161-1912.1998.tb00204.x)

12) Hammond, W. R., & Yung, B. (1993). Psychology's role in the public health response to assaultive violence among young African-American men. American Psychologist, 48(2), 142–154. https://doi.org/10.1037/0003-066X.48.2.142

13) Rahn Kennedy Bailey, Holly L. Blackmon, Francis L. Stevens, Major Depressive Disorder in the African American Population: Meeting the Challenges of Stigma, Misdiagnosis, and Treatment Disparities, Journal of the National Medical Association, Volume 101, Issue 11, 2009, Pages 1084-1089, ISSN 0027-9684, https://doi.org/10.1016/S0027-9684(15)31102-0.